THE GREAT AMERICAN LONELINESS

Other works by Peter Najarian

Voyages
Wash Me On Home, Mama
Daughters of Memory

THE GREAT AMERICAN LONELINESS

By Peter Najarian

BLUE CRANE BOOKS
WATERTOWN, MASSACHUSETTS

THE GREAT AMERICAN LONELINESS
BY PETER NAJARIAN

First Published in 1999 by
Blue Crane Books
P.O.Box 291, Cambridge, MA 02238

First Edition
1   3   5   7   9   10   8   6   4   2

Cover painting and Illustrations by Peter Najarian
Book design, typography & electronic pagination by
Arrow Graphics, Inc. Watertown, Massachusetts
Printed in Canada

Library of Congress Cataloging-in-Publication Data
Najarian, Peter, 1940–
The great American loneliness / by Peter Najarian.—1st ed.
        p.   cm.
ISBN 1-886434-09-3 (alk. paper)
1. Najarian, Peter, 1940–   .
2. Authors, American—20th century—Biography.
3. Oakland (Calif.)—Intellectual life.
4. Armenian Americans—Biography.
I. Title.
PS3564.A5Z47   1999
813' .54—dc21   99–18076
        [b]   CIP

What is the price of Experience? do men
        buy it for a song?
Or wisdom for a dance in the street? No, it is
        bought with the price
Of all that a man hath, his house, his wife, his
        children.
Wisdom is sold in the desolate market where
        none come to buy,
And in the wither'd field where the farmer
        plows for bread in vain.

from Enion's Lament in the *Four Zoas*,
by William Blake

    There is no question of failure. It is like traveling a long and arduous road in an unknown country. Of all the innumerable steps there is only the last which brings you to your destination. Yet you will not consider previous steps as failures. Each brought you nearer to your goal, even when you had to turn back to bypass an obstacle. In reality each step brings you to your goal because to be always on the move, learning, discovering, unfolding, is your eternal destiny. Living is life's only purpose. The Self does not identify itself with success or failure—the very idea of becoming this or that is unthinkable. The Self understands that success and failure are relative, that they are the very warp and weft of life. Learn from both and go beyond. If you have not learned, repeat.

from the dialogues with Nisargadatta in *I Am That*.

CONTENTS

THE GREAT AMERICAN LONELINESS

FOR MY FRIENDS

I've been writing since boyhood and my work was first published in the Rutgers magazine, *Anthologist*, the editors my friends Jim Mohan, Alan Cheuse and Robert Pinsky. Then my friend, Richard Yates, got a short work published in the Macmillan anthology, *New Voices*, and this would grow into a book called *Voyages*, which my friend, Norm Fruchter, helped get published at Pantheon Books. Jack Antreassian later reprinted it at Ararat Press.

My second book, *Wash Me On Home Mama*, was written in the first half of the Seventies, and my friends at the Berkeley Poets Co-op published it with their small press.

The first two narratives in this book are from an unpublished book I wrote in Detroit in the second half of the Seventies. The Co-op later published *The Story* in their *Anthology*, and my friend, Margot Pepper, got *India* into *Five Fingers Review*.

Puer Eternis was written while I was visiting my friend, Gatz Hjorstberg, in Montana. My friend, Daniel Rudman, had asked me to write it for his basketball anthology, *Take It To The Hoop*, and years later I sent it to my friend, Al Zolynas, who published it in his and Fred Moramarco's anthology, *Men Of Our Time*.

In the beginning of the Eighties I wrote a novel called *Daughters Of Memory*, which I published with my friend,

Mike Helm, who ran a small press out of his basement a few blocks from me.

In the meantime I started learning how to paint, thanks to my cousin, Ashod Pinajian, and my friend, Lenny Silverberg.

I wrote only journals while learning how to paint, then in '87 my friend Peter Stine asked me to write my Big Game story for his anthology, *The Sixties*.

After I returned from Armenia in '89 I wrote about it in a memoir called *Hishadag*, which my friend, Leo Hamalian, later published in *Ararat Magazine*. The opening section had been about Amsterdam, and after Leo left it out I combined it with two other sections into what is now called *The Girl*.

After *Hishadag* I wrote a book which never got published, and then I wrote *The Aki*, a short work about my mother's childhood, which my friend, David Kherdian, published in his magazine, *Forkroads*.

Then came a dark and painful time when I felt my life's work had come to nothing, and out of this darkness I wrote *Harvest*, which my friend, Dobby Boe, later published in his magazine, *Writing On The Edge*.

A short while later Peter Stine heard from our mutual friend, John Ruhlman, about my sub job in Oakland, and Peter asked me to write about it for his anthology, *American Cities*, so I wrote and sent him *Window Into Eden*.

Then one day three years ago, Bob Blauner asked me to write something about my mother for his anthology, *Our Mother's Spirit*. I told him I was tired of writing about my mother, so he taped an interview. I didn't like the interview and rewrote it into what was recently published as *The Artist's Mother* in Bob's new book. This portrait of my mother and the one about her childhood developed into a long work which is too long for a small press and which I

will try to publish with a big one. To end this book I sliced
away one of the sections and called it *America*.

About a year ago David Kherdian sent me his new work
published by a small press, Blue Crane Books. I had by now
collected my shorter works, so with David's reference I sent
them to Alvart Badalian at Blue Crane, who was receptive
but whose distributor didn't project enough sales to cover
the cost. Ten years ago The Alex Manoogian Cultural Fund
had given me a grant to help publish *Daughters Of Memory*,
so I asked Louise Manoogian Simone, who chairs the fund,
to help me again, which she has done very generously and
for which of course I am deeply grateful.

Like all artists I have always written and painted
because I needed to, and with this need came the one to be
heard and seen. The first need is part of what we call the
soul and the second of the self, the first is with love and the
second for love, like the *in* and *for itself* in philosophy, the
first unmanifest without the second striving. When I make
lines there is no loneliness and my *I* seems in service to my
fingers and my breath, then comes the loneliness when my
I is in command with all its longing and hunger.

This loneliness is not just "American" of course, but of
a universal nature, or what we call the self's search for the
soul, yet it comes dressed in a culture, which is why the editor, Seymour Lawrence, said of Richard Brautigan, "He
died of The Great American Loneliness," perhaps quoting
Kerouac or Fitzgerald, America a name for our own particular kind of journey. When I was young I used this name for
the cause of my personal suffering, as if it were an enemy to
what my ideal America was supposed to be, and when I lived
in England I felt more natural as an alien than feeling one
in the land where I was born. My parents had found refuge
here, but I grew up longing for a home I imagined in their
childhood. I had a promising future in England, but I
returned to the States and found myself in what Blake once

described as a "desolate market" in which my need to write was in conflict with my other needs.

Yet, as Blake said, there is no progression without contraries, and my work was forged in this conflict, which became the only subject I really cared about. I needed to write, yet I felt I had nothing to write about but a formless longing, so I had to find my subjects as best I could and trust my fingers and breath to lead the way. In the meantime I remained in an America where I felt I had failed to find a place, for aside from the small advance for *Voyages* and two awards I earned nothing from writing except a few lecturing jobs, and my average income was never above the poverty line. Yet it was my so-called failure that fed my writing as if they were the same like a snake that eats its tail. I felt like an artist starving not for food but a home and family, and I thought my failure was the cause. Then I realized I was not really starving but in love, and it was this love of making lines that kept me searching for my true subject, for I was in love not only with my soul but how it was mirrored in my friends who are my true America, my mother the most important of all. It is to them I dedicate this humble book.

Berkeley and Fresno,
Spring '98

THE STORY

One night, deep in the old black hole, I looked for a story to take me away, but there was only the usual stuff, Aeschylus and Tolstoy and so forth. Dozens of heroes lay on my floor like the human condition, and I prowled through them like an ant in my pubic hair in search of something, food, love, an orgasm, another ant, who knows what? So did I search until hero after hero lay defeated by my loneliness, the Vikings, Bodley Heads and Modern Library Giants all staring up from my battlefield. "Tell me what you want," Balzac said, "and I'll write it, guaranteed." "Be with yourself," Pascal commanded, "and face the music." I couldn't take it anymore and came here

to you. Once again it was three o'clock in the morning, but this time I was full of peanut butter and pumpernickel, so I wasn't going to kill myself. Here now, a fat moon setting as the sun rises, I'm still looking for a story and this time it has a man and a woman.

The man is at that round and even age of forty when everything must be okay, and he's a painter, a house painter and a art painter who lives with the pigeons and the factories in what we call our great achievement, the city in history, or West Berkeley, California, in the years before the gentry arrive. He lives alone in an old balloon-frame house and the neighbors raise chickens across the yard, the low rent like a subsidy and he himself eccentric like a wobbly ball with a nipple.

The woman however is at the crooked age of thirty-one when nothing is ever right. She works for the Post Office collecting mail part-time, and she's as lonely as a frog in a bathtub looking for someone to help her out, then returning to her piano she pours her longing like a diary of clouds and the notes purl from her window with no one but the squirrel waving a tail for an encore.

The man's name is Harry, but the woman's name is uncertain, since she always wants more than one, like Tapa or Parvati or Vartanoosh. Her real name is Nana but it's never enough, and her hair (as she looks in the mirror her hair comes first) is also never absolute and perfect. Shoulder length and tawny with a dash of red, it's never full enough and she's going to cut it one of these days, even though she wants to hide her ears. She's vain as hell and hates her nose which always fails like her porcelain in the ceramics class, yet her lips are okay, good standard kissable lips when she's in a good mood, and her teeth are regular with a sexy gap. Her eyes, her eyes however, are what she looks at when she wants to love herself, her eyes are what she wants her name to resemble, they are so innocent though they cut like ammonia when she's in a pissy mood. Maybe I should call her Dolores.

Harry could be called Buster or Izzy or any name like a junkyard bargain or a hearty cockroach, yet Harry will do, Cockroach Harry, the lunatic. There's a Turkish saying, *for the lunatic everyday is a holiday*, and if you think not of those who mumble in laundromats but of hobos and gurus, you will see my Harry lost in a dandelion or a chicken turd or whatever comes into his visionary happiness. Dolores is always detailed and never leaves a pimple unpopped, but Harry is universal like an egg lying naked in the middle of the yard, his baldness like a tonsure and his nose prehistoric, his eyes like pebbles under water and his ears always growing with succulent lobes. He's not ugly, but he could never look like the macho Dolores wants to fall in love with, especially with his socks slipping below his ankles. If there's anything she can't abide in a man it's shameful socks, yet despite his lumpiness, he's no noodle and can glow with a soft light like the aftermath of rain when the phallic mushrooms are dewy luminous.

So now we have Harry and What's Her Name, and the narrator of course is this I who is always different from you, and who you are is why I am writing. And the scene is in the city and like all cities it has a road to the "country," which is where Dolores is always longing to live. She would give anything to live in that Eden without streetlights and her bedroom walls that never sing, anything except her longing itself which keeps her here like the string of a red balloon. Melancholy on a hill in the middle of her collection route, the sundown and the smog a dramatic orange, she looks out to the *country* with her longing for a macho and a baby and the Whole Earth Catalogue, the aspen quivering in the breeze and a monthly royalty check in a mossy mailbox. *Someday*, she hopes, *someday*. But me, I'm sick of that theme. *Let's all go to the country and live with Tibetan sourdough and tomato chutney*. Well, go ahead, go live out there, go piss under the fir trees and leave the city to the slobs, yet she doesn't, she stays here, for after all, she is my character, and wherever she goes she will always be longing until I find a happy ending.

Harry however loves wherever he is. Here on the other side of the tracks with the mice cozy behind the refrigerator, he eats a quiet bowl of porridge while the semi-trailers roar like a juggernaut past his window.

"You want some?"

No sugar or even yinny syrup, just plain gooey egg-mule oatmeal like semen with a dab of margarine.

"I love it."

He finishes the bowl and sits back and looks at his hands as if they just returned from a long vacation.

"I've been eating it all my life."

Back to Michiko who is frying her celery root and not listening to the same old news on the people-supported station, a full moon rising over the hills and her tofu stir-fry sprinkled with soy sauce, her green tea brewing in superb ceramic and her Zen kitchen in kindergarten yellows and blues and a careful red. Ah, Michy, you got everything going for you, you got taste, you got looks, you even got a little money, but Jesus are you fussy. What was the matter with that guy at the party last night, what was his name?

"Melvin."

Yes, Melvin, what was the matter with Melvin, he had a good face and nice socks and he wanted to have dinner with you tonight, wouldn't it have been more Reichian if you were eating with Melvin instead of alone?

"He wore after-shave lotion."

But it smelled okay.

"It smelled like after-shave lotion."

Ah, Michy.

"Don't call me Michy!"

I don't know what I'm going to do with her. She becomes so knotted I want to pull her open from her neck to her crotch. She's been sleeping alone for two years and her bed feels like Emily Dickinson. How she'll get together with Harry I don't know. He's seen her around lots of times and she's seen him too but never noticed of course. Once he was standing in front of her in the Co-op and I told him to turn and give her one of his oatmeal smiles, but she couldn't see him because she was staring at a zenith of masculinity buying imported beer down the aisle.

So here now in the middle of bamboo shoots and broccoli she's crying again, the old crying of the ages trickling with a few tears and then gushing up until she's so soaked with misery there's nothing I can do. Help her, Harry, don't just stand there with your damn pencil!

But he ignores me. He's at his table by the window while the Amtrak rolls by, his baldness mooning under the lamp like an indecent exhibition. Since he's ambidextrous he can draw each hand and once again they swallow his eyes in the hatching and hairs like creatures of the deep in psychedelic hallucinations, his hands that seem not to belong to him but are his friends like a pair of *naga* buddies.

"Rocco and Lefty."

He pays homage by drawing them after dinner every evening, his hands that can create a world like a dreaming god, their quiet fingers never ceasing to prey upon anything that can be seen or imagined, everywhere food for their omnivorous writhing.

He draws them in the same flow of slimy samsara as the one in which he eats his porridge or masturbates, but Cynthia alone in her bed, well, she has her own kind of kundalini. She wouldn't mind me describing her sex life, but I mustn't do it like a talk show about vibrators. Lying in bed caressing herself, she agrees it may be vegetotherapeutic and relaxing, but it is still part of the darkness after shutting the lamp and only the darkness matters now, all her orgone energy going to waste. She can't face it and buries her eyes in the pillow and even tries to pray as if a you is listening. I am here, I want to tell her, but it doesn't seem to matter and she is crying again. It's okay, dear girl, you can cry now, it's okay to cry.

THE GREAT AMERICAN LONELINESS

Noon the next day and Harry can't get his painting right, landscape with figures too ambitious once again.

"It'll work out."

But when? There's not much time left and when he dies the Salvation Army will sell his work for seventy-five cents.

"What a bargain! A masterpiece for seventy-five cents."

His eyeballs roll at the thought of an old black lady buying it with some plastic fruit and hanging it in her kitchen, *Six nudes With Trees And Rocks*.

"She'll love it, every day when she's lonely she'll look at my picture and I'll be with her, that's what art is, Sonny Boy."

But what old black lady is going to buy a five by four canvas full of genitals and hang it in her kitchen?

"You're right, it's too big, I'll cut a couple of feet off the side and another at the bottom, I couldn't get those parts right anyway."

He was always like this, ever since he was a kid in love with the odor of gum turpentine, he too always wanting to paint like the little Dutch boy in blue overalls. Here now he is actually doing it.

"The success."

And yet he never made it above the poverty line, he never made anything.

"I made the Honor Roll."

It was not enough and yet he still feels as good as Degas singing an aria while the model waited.

Even Mildred feels good this morning. She woke with her dreams still weighing on her like the cat, but then she became vertical and ate both halves of the grapefruit and played some Brahms and Satchmo. Her friend Sally Moonglow dropped by and the two of them drank French Roast in the garden and gossiped about friends from the old days, one friend leading to another from Hoboken to Spitalfields until Sally had to pick up her child from the

Montessori school, a spinster left staring at the towhee on the plum branch. All those friends were almost a family, but as she looks through her empty cottage there seems no one left, not even Sally whom she hardly sees anymore. Where did she go wrong, how come she doesn't have a child in a Montessori?

Meanwhile Harry's eyes are zooming everywhere like fearless blue-bottles crazy with space, the garbage can leading to the fuschia bells and the fuschia bells to the chickens and the chickens on and on until he has another masterpiece, everywhere he looks another masterpiece, even cigarette butts in a Greyhound urinal or his morning deposit in the toilet bowl.

But Jennifer doesn't buy that kind of samsara, no, to her everything has to look right and all socks have to be straight. She was always this way, even as a child with her bed next to the bureau and the bureau next to the bookcase and it better not be dusty either. She hated ugliness, there was no excuse for it, the crippled and poor were excused, but astroturf and Las Vegas were not tolerated. Unable to banish them from the universe she withdrew into her cottage and filled it like a museum, never leaving it without dressing to kill, like now as she walks to work with her back straight as if she were in a Samurai movie.

When she arrives at the Post Office annex she climbs up the dock and pushes through the swing doors and then slips her time card in the slot and collects her keys from the clerk in the cage, then in her snazzy half-ton she is no longer the cry of the ages but *The Mail Carrier*, a varsity member of the human race, always on time.

Here she comes, right-hand drive up the avenue like Amelia Earhart, her hair in a bun with an ivory spike and her corduroys tight and tough, her hands calloused and heroic. Brake, stop, jump out and swing the great key chain like Forties bebop, then flip open box, stuff letters in sack, slam lid locked and hop back in van, perfecto!

She circles the city like a prima donna of the streets while everyone shouts and claps hoorah, for she is one of them now, a hermes of communication, a part of the cosmic design, not some masturbating spinster eating tofu every night, no, she is now a homosapien first class, a potential Buddha!

After her first swing she takes her break in the basement lounge of the Main Office and bullthrows with whoever happens to be there. The lighting is like an old Polish movie and the walls vomit green, but it's not really ugly, it's as dull as a conger eel and as sad as a lobotomy, but wherever she looks there may be a Ph.D. in medieval French or an assorted kook or nouveau poor. In the rest of the day she can be Anna Karenina, but here now she's at home in the world with her feet on a chair, laughing with Jackpot, the maintenance man.

"How's the piana?" he says with his hot dog and mustard breath.

He likes her. He doesn't see a neurotic snob but a woman who likes to laugh and who likes him. How could she not like him, his old skin and hard life like G major, his socks curling below his ankles as she stamps him approved, *noble human being.*

"Well, I got to mosey along," he says.

"So long, Jackpot."

We're getting closer. If she can enjoy Jackpot then it's not far to Harry.

He's just around the corner from the annex, but she doesn't see him inside when she passes his window, his brush still pecking like a rooster as if he were a giant cock copulating with the world, his multitude of nudes and landscapes stacked for the old Black Lady who will hang them by her garbage can after he dies. He has painted hard all day and here he is still struggling against his old enemy of the night.

"That Which Doesn't Come Out Right."

Doesn't he care about anything else, doesn't he want a wife and a child, why is he like this?

"Maybe it's a plot."

It doesn't matter anymore, it's too late to go to graduate school and he tries some zinc yellow instead.

Meanwhile Bernadette is worrying about her car and can't decide whether to have it fixed or buy another one. She doesn't really need a car, but without one she will be like those who must ask for a ride when there's a good time in the hills. Asking for anything after the age of thirty is dangerous and time is running out, she has to decide, if she has a car she will be an adult, yet without one she will be ecological and public. She decides not to decide and pay the fine to the Motor Vehicle Bureau.

The days pass until Harry finally puts his brush down, for even he wears out. He can't paint anymore and he just stares at the wall. He has been staring at walls all his life and the time has come for them to crack. It is just a little crack like a hair on his nose, but it's enough for him to slip inside like he would do as a child in the wall by his bed. Exhausted and dreamy, he closes his eyes and slips into the crack of his life like a little boy walking home through a vision, the slit opening into an infinite cave with the sky for a ceiling and the ground a shore by peaceful combers, the stars of palm leaves swaying in the breeze like hula dancers.

It is the cave of art and on its magic carpet lie the heroes of its epic, Ox-eyed Rembrandt with his arm around Michelangelo the Cloud King, Gauguin of the Flashing Eyes in a jig with Pablo of the Nimble Wits, Wind-Swift Degas of the Fleet Foot singing with Piero the Giant-Killer and Ma Yuan in a duet with Barrel-Chested Phidias, the carpet rolling on to include the rest of them, Senmut and the sculptors of Ellora and all those all the way back to the bison on the limestone, a little visitor moving between them like his life unrolling for review.

"Whatsamatta, kid?" Fra Angelico asks him. *"He wants zi place on zi rug,"* says Rodin. *"Vell,"* says Breughal, *"does he haf da right papers?"* "He don' need no papers," Valesquez says, *"the keed's okay."* "Sure," says Giorgione, *"but he needa sometin'."*

What, what does he need to join them? He could draw well enough, though not as well as Picasso of course, and though he hasn't suffered as much as Van Gogh it has been enough, so what has always kept him off the rug? He squints hard to see its pattern and he finds an Old Black Kali dumping his work in the thursday morning garbage truck.

In the meantime something has happened to Brenda since she has decided not to decide, and it has been like mini letting-go. Today, the temperature between fifty and sixty and the barometer at forty percent, Mars passing Pollux, Saturn, and Regulus, she is suddenly dancing so lively her cat runs behind the bathtub. She could play the piano or sew zafus or do anything with her hands, yet she had always felt awkward dancing. Because she's svelte and. . . .

"You mean skinny."

Svelte, not skinny, svelte. As I was saying, since she's svelte and willowy, her movements once felt stiff, but her breath sinks deeper now and it inflates her slimness until her long limbs seem to sway like a dancing elephant. The deep crying has stretched her sternocleidomastoids and her masseters and the superficial abductors of her upper thighs which had always kept her legs pressed together, in other words she is ready now to love someone and be loved. Little does she know, however, who her future honeybunch will be.

But in the meantime he has sunk even deeper into his old bumpy couch, his weariness curling him into a slurpy nap which will leave his shirt sleeve wet with spittle. He feels drowsy when he wakes and he calls upon his two buddies to revive him.

"Rocco? Lefty?"

Well, my two characters are just about to get together for a happy ending, and it will have to happen soon before my unemployment checks run out. But in what laundromat or dentist's office will they come together? Millions try every day and some even have children and pansies and still can't make a happy ending, is there any happy ending before the Black Lady weaves her necklace of skulls?

Harry can't paint anymore, though the weather has become his favorite skies of windswept clouds and sycamore leaves waltzing over the sidewalks. He tries to draw them but his two buddies are gone and he leaves the house like a blind Degas at the end of his life riding busses all day.

The rainy season has started to wane but it's still too early for housepainting, and as the days pass he wanders under the blossoming plum and acacia, the green hills rolling into the Gate like a uroborus who eats its tail. One afternoon he was in the underground BART station and the platform was crowded with mascara and mustaches in the prime of life, and a man was eating a candy bar like a paragon of evolution. He was a beautiful man with a briefcase and a haircut, yet as Harry studied this sentient being he saw him swallowed in the black hole that lay ahead, all candy bars and Vermeers doomed to the five-twenty train that would arrive at any minute.

Yet Esther's been getting better and her arms no longer ask what to do when she thrusts her pelvis and lifts her elbows, her breasts stretching as if she were finally proud of them. As if in an Armenian *hantess*, she claps her hands in front of her face and again over her head and then clicking her thumbs she flips her head and kicks, *"Hadee Yalah!"*

That a baby, Manooshag! Yes, she has bought another car! A Volvo! She is no longer a Bug! At first she was not sure, the Volkswagon was so frugal and tidy and even the name of this new car sounded as tubby as a tuba, but then she realized she didn't want to be a Mary Poppins anymore, no, now she would now be a Volvo like a successful chiropractor, a ten year old one but a Volvo nevertheless. Even the daffodils were in bloom in her garden. Something is going to happen, she can feel it up her spine and she's not going to hold it down anymore, no, alone or not alone she is going to do it, she is going to be happy, she is going to get the hell out of her bedroom.

She decided last night as she lay awake listening to the old tom who wanted her Boops-Boops. He was so loud and horny she had to get up to chase him away, but he just crouched under the bamboo like the *elan vital*, his ear chewed and his face scarred like a Beethoven who won't give up. She had always thought of him as a disgusting old lecher, but closer now than she had ever been to him she was humbled by his mission. Who did she think she was, he seemed to say, a fussy human in a nightgown trying to keep him from the big bang?

Meanwhile Harry is still wandering like Gauguin asking why and what for? Tomorrow he would still be alive and unable to paint he would still have to keep living. Why live if he can't paint? If he goes on like this he'll start eating it like Vincent. Then walking around the campus one day he passes the ride board on the way to a men's room and he sees a little bird that has been drawn with one of those new "razor-point" felt tips. It's a copy from the T'zu Chow style, around 14th Century, and he stops to admire it.

Underneath it says, *Rider Wanted to Montana. Share Gas and Driving, Nana, 548-1407*

Yes, it's spring, and her strawberry patch has little white blossoms. Tired from digging in the garden all day, she's decides to reward herself by eating out. She's just about to step in the shower when the phone rings and a voice like Jimmy Durante's asks her if she's "the Nana going to Montana." She tells him she would like to meet him but she's going out to eat in a few minutes.

"Oh, yeh," he says, "Where's that?"

"At a little Japanese place."

"Terrific," he says, "Do they serve oatmeal?"

He waits on the corner and when she sees him she says to herself, *No, I'm not, no.* And this even after he trimmed his ears and wore his best sweatshirt, yet she sees only the kind of face she has ignored all her life and here it was with nine hundred miles and a night in a motel, a face like a tired monk facing the wall all night.

Then suddenly he walks up to her and lifts his eyebrows like enlightenment. It's him, she recognizes him immediately, the one she's been struggling for all her life like Uma for Siva or Loretta Young for Spencer Tracy in a Depression romance. I always wanted to be in love and here my characters will finally make it.

"Hello," she says, "I'm Nana."

Perfect! With just the right modesty and *nil admirari*.

"Hello, Nana," he says with a twinkle in his nose, his

hands coming alive and wanting to paint the cleavage in her teeth, "I'm Harry."

She can't resist. This is Jackpot and Johannes Brahms all rolled into one.

Inside the Ozu Cafe the owner's little boy is at one of the tables scribbling his homework while watching *Startrek* on a little black and white. The owner, a tortured woman who is always smiling, bows and pours the tea, the sundown sliced by the blinds and turning everywhere to gold, Harry and Nana sitting back to watch Mr. Spock and Mr. Kirk have an argument while the little boy is like an oriental cupid about to shoot them with sandalwood and pachouli oil. Then the smiling tortured woman returns.

"Some saki, please," Harry says, as if he were President of Toyota. Nana is impressed. She could have children with this guy, there's potential in those earlobes.

But as the Buddha says, the end of living is dying and no movie lasts forever, a month or a year or at most two or seven, then it's back to oatmeal and tofu. There will be good times, yes, there will be moments when they lie in a tent and listen to the thunder and kiss each other like chipmunks, moments when they drive through the night reciting auto-biographies or copulating like whales in a resounding abun-dance, moments they will want to share with even Caligulas and Hitlers as if to cure them, yet all these moments will pass and they will part or be parted and become like drift-wood in each other's memory, for no love story can survive the Black Lady.

I don't care, she thinks, she wants it again though she will suffer when it's gone, she wants it to grow inside her this time, she wants this man across the tiny dish of pickled cabbage, this funny man with juicy earlobes.

No, I have failed again, I don't have the right ending.

"Make it witty and sell it to the *New Yorker*," says my Grandpa on the wall.

"I don't know how, Grandpa."

"You don't know how? You know how to write fifteen manila folders full of horseshit and you don't know how to write one little story that will sell?"

"It takes a special knack."

"I knack your head off, knack, don't give me any knacks, sell something by April fifteenth or get a job."

His Nietzche mustache has no pity for my old Underwood. His children slaughtered and his grandchildren scattered from Bellport to Fresno, he scowls at my failure.

"Stop fooling around, make money and have kids, enough of this art crap sitting here staring at pigeons every day. Do you think Tolstoy stared at pigeons all day? Are you a writer or pigeon-keeper?"

He's right, it's either selling this or food stamps for the rest of my life. But will my Harry and Nana be doomed to another folder? Will no one but a reject editor read this? You don't answer of course, you've never answered nor have you cared whether I make a dust jacket or not, all you care about is that I keep sitting here like an old seamstress sewing lines all day, my bin full of dresses for women I will never know, you, always you and your pigeons, you to whom I have been writing since a summer on the chicken farm when there were no other kids around, you in the clouds above the river and the river itself, the old Fatso of the tugboat disappearing in the bay, you, always you and the Black Lady.

In the meantime, Rocco and Lefty are throbbing with desire to reach over the soy sauce and touch the new woman with the sexy gap. Harry hasn't felt this excited since he first discovered Borobodur, his hands coiling the pellucid noodles in the norikabe as if drawing her a valentine. Then after the fortune cookies the red sky fills him with adventure and he wants to drive across the bridge and lick a mocha fudge together as they stroll around the fishing boats.

"Okay, Harold," she says.

And that's it, March 21, 1976, seven forty seven p.m. in the Ozu Cafe. No one has ever called him Harold before.

And so her chubby Volvo carries them across the low tide of a full moon and the great pylons open to the lineaments of gratified desire, Nana sitting back after asking him to drive and her hand wanting to reach up his sweatshirt to tickle his nipples. *My darling, Harold*, she whispers to herself, *my dearest*.

And so everything is going to be okay, food stamps or no food stamps. She will clean his house and burn incense and he will cook her *lachmajoon*. He will be able to paint again and she will play Coltrane while he does her portrait. They will live together four days a week and miss each other the other three and when she returns from her travels she will sneak around his easel and hug him like a watermelon. Then they will lie in bed with their wrinkled genitals glued to each other like pachyderms and in the morning his tender arm will feel like a elephant's trunk across her breasts. He will paint her and draw her again and again like Degas' bathers and Rembrandt's wives and she will pose at her piano or by dancing like Khajuraho. They will fight, of course, but it will be more like basketball than Hiroshima and they will each discover the other's childhood in the meantime. Then they will walk along the bay and watch the egret glide across the estuary and after the puppy will come their first baby and then the second and then the third, their sex life deepening until they commingle like Blake's eternals at the end of a prophecy. Then they will die like Grandma Moses and El Greco's old man in the Met, wrinkled and glowing in the old black hole like natural childbirth, nothing impossible for my two characters, as long as I'm here writing to you, pigeons or no pigeons.

INDIA

When she was a child one summer on a cousin's chicken farm, she wanted to pick tomatoes with the migrants across the road and to watch them play dominoes in the shack with the door open. Theirs was supposed to be the hard life like the Depression tales of denim and calico, the hard life was a term like *wisdom* or *hero* and it belonged to wobblies and bindlestiffs who lived by campfires with potatoes all the time. Then she grew up and got a job in Harlem. She had often been unhappy, but the hard life was different from her unhappiness and she could escape Harlem anytime by subway or bus. In India there was no escape.

She had come here wanting to die. She had come wanting to enter a darkness as if it were a garbage can in the childhood basement she had always feared, she had wanted it to swallow her like a Persephone in the furnace with the ashes in a bucket by the door. *Come*, said the tiger in the airline ad, *India is waiting*, and she had bought a one way fare as if she would never return.

Here now on her map near the end of journey, the subcontinent is like a heart stained with iodine and curry and her route a vein from temples to caves. In the bungalow toilet the water dribbles down her thigh after she washes her anus and rinses her fingers in her little bowl. Her diarrhea is gone and her turds are firm, so there's just a speck in the water. In a village in Goa they had dropped through a shute and pig came to devour them in the yard. She had always looked for a clean toilet and could never do it in the open like that lovely woman who lifted her sari and squatted in the middle of a field, her cheeks glowing in the long rays of an early sun and her deposit like lucre.

She had come to India to die and it showed how to squat like a human being and never need a seat again. She had come to India to escape her life and it made her touch her shit and clean herself with her own fingers. As she sits under a banyan tree a parrot flashes from its branch and a leper begs beneath the aerobatic roots. When she starts to sketch them another group of children approach for another backshish.

Backshish, *backshish*, they cry, their hands out for some paisa or even a rupee, more than the doby would earn in a day smacking laundry on a rock. She pours coins in their palms and they disappear behind an old ox munching banana peels amid the beeping traffic, a girl picking lice from her mother's hair and another patting pancakes of dung on the wall to dry, a barefoot boy watching the buffalo nearby.

When he sees the notebook he approaches like a wary kitten, his eyes adorable in his dusty face and his rags one wouldn't in America even use to wash a floor.

"Come here," she says, "come closer." Is he right handed, and yet what difference does it make, he holds the pen as if it is an egg or a garter snake.

"Here, let me guide your hand," she says. It is callused and tender at the same time. With her other arm around his shoulder she wants to hold his sweetness as long as she can, but he pulls away when the drawing is finished. It is a copy from a scroll painting by Li Ti.

"Holy cow!" he babbles in his dialect, and he runs to show his sister who is patting shitcakes on the wall.

In the meantime another young woman in a ragged sari walks by like a queen with a basket of junk on her head and rings on her filthy toes, a child slung at her side sucking her nipple and the others lagging as she yells at them to hurry. Where are they going into the night, the blue landscape haloed with lanterns in the open tents and the families huddled in shawls like Christmas mangers?

In Benares the next day it is Christmas eve and bathtime in the holy waters. As she walks along the shore she steps around the castles of shit and watches a westerner dive in. "Drink it," he says, "it cures you of everything."

The great Ganga where the dead are oiled and burned, all except infants and untouchables and holy men and cows, the uncremated dumped midstream where little sharks are said to purify them. On the stone steps of a shitty ruin a sick old monkey with a bald belly and big red testicles sits waiting for his end, his tiny eyes staring back from his animal innocence.

She walks upstream and passes a skinny *sadhu* and a chubby merchant who lather their balls under loincloth and underwear, the light now crimson and gold as if to reveal the secret of India's power, a cow head floating in the brown waves and a hustler rowing a tourist in a dinghy to the other shore, a small boy slapping his buffalo into a bath and the huge animal bowing its horns like a great samurai to a little emperor, a young woman washing her hair like a royal dancer and swinging it in the air while garlands of marigolds float from a corpse on the shore, its arm collapsing in a flaming pyre. Swallows dive and vanish in the glowing dusk and a full moon is rising in the sundown, someone in the distance is playing a flute and the notes purl into the dying monkey and the bathing woman and the boy and the buffalo and the merchant and the *sadhu* and the burning corpse, the music rising and falling with the luminous waves as if from their birth in the mountain snow to their death in the green delta.

"*Boum Shankar! Siva Shankar!*" everyone shouts in a houseboat that night, a *chillum* of hashish raised above their heads in praise of the Great Lord. They are Johnny from Florida who smuggled hashish from Manali so he could stay longer, and Geta from Japan on the road since he was fifteen, Anita from Germany on her way to a guru and Toby from Australia on her summer vacation, their passports around their necks like swans or roaches and their routes interweaving from hostel to hut to just a blanket on the sand, the lines on their maps like graphs of proud adventures.

They move on to a basement and pass the *chillum* like a peace pipe to the natives who have brought some instruments. One of the natives is supposed to be a priest and he places the little phallus and vulva of a *shivalingam* in the center of the circle by the candles. Then the music begins and the chanting of the *hari-rama*, soft and slow at first and then faster and louder in the rhythm rising from the memory of Ginsberg and Orlavsky in a protest during the war.

"*Rama hari, Krishna hari, hari Rama. . . .*"

Over and over and louder and faster, the shadows dancing on the wall from the flickering candles and the syllables humming in the silence at the end. Then Johnny turns to the priest with the bells and asks, "May I have them, please?" The priest nods sideways in his Indian yes and that's when the *sadhu* walks in with his trident and pail and wearing only mala beads and loin cloth, his face smeared vermillion and his body white with ash.

The *sadhu* sits next to Johnny like an old wino in full lotus, Johnny now jingling the bells very softly and whispering an ancient chant from America. It is *Jingle Bells* and his voice is like an echo as he closes his eyes and sings slowly, his hashish accent like a primal rhythm from the world of stockings by a fireplace.

"Jing el bells, jing el bells, jing el. . . ."

All the way back to a childhood evening walking home in the snow and a peek at the footmarks as if a ghost will disappear before it can be seen.

"Oh what fun it is to ride. . . ."

Through the whole verse and then again as if it is an American *hari-rama*, the *sadhu* waving his head and chanting as best he can the strange syllables of this new mantra from the west, the chanting growing louder and louder.

"In a one horse open sleigh eh. . . ."

Everyone bobbing behind the reins of their abandoned breath, the unenlightened Johnny who misses his girlfriend and Mr. Anonymous who sleeps in a graveyard, America and tantra finally united.

"*Om Nama Siva Om,*" the *sadhu* chants, and she wants to move closer to him, she wanted to know his secret, who is he, doesn't he want a home and family, isn't he scared without health insurance? He leaves as he came with no forwarding address.

Stoned and hungry, she wanders with Johnny and Geta into the ancient city as if it is a Bethlehem of epiphanies, the sudden cows emerging from the shadows like phantoms from prehistory and the labyrinth of neolithic lanes like the mews of time itself.

Then they stop to eat pastry at a colorful shop with music in the rear, then at another shop to eat curd in the clay cups they throw in the gutter, earth to earth, then she drops her pen in the gutter and fishes it from the mire and does not wash her hands. She is tired of washing her hands and squeezing iodine in her water. In the lantern glimmer of the cobbled lane she watches a goat lick a puddle by a water pump and a man pump into a pail like life itself teeming in the gravid coils of an ancient hive, animal life and yoghurt life endlessly eating while Johnny talks about his job in a butcher shop and Geta about a monastery in Rajgir where he will meditate without food or water for a week. "You want to come?" Geta asks. "I may come for a visit," she says.

But she will have her own kind of fast. Does it come from the hashish pipe which she did not smoke through a circle of her thumb like the others, or is it from the gutter and not washing her hands? It is from the great Siva himself like a gift from the *sadhu*. The hotel manager has seen it many times.

"Don't worry," he says, his face vague in the blur of delirium, "it is only a bug of some sort. Where are you from? Do you know Detroit? I have a cousin in Detroit."

A wave of her hand makes him go away. "Don't be afraid," he says as he leaves, "it is only a bug of some sort."

Yet there is no fear but only delirium and the wish to disappear in it. No fear, no longing, no future, no life, the fantasy come true of a derelict in a flophouse indifferent to the mice and the man pissing against the wall in the lane outside. No more journey or decisions but just waiting to vomit the bile of her life as if the bug in her belly had spewed a dinghy for her soul, the bumpy bed bobbing on the throbbing river of fever and chills and a host of bogies swelling in the candleflame like flashbacks to genocide and plague and the dying spider monkey and burning corpse, the flotsam of a family album swirling in a crawl to the toilet like the uncremated dumped midstream. She is finally one of them, their crusted lips and empty eyes her mirror in the glowing Atlantis of delirium, the jeweled domes of ancient temples shredding into flashing scales of a butchered fish and the effluvia of history, her eyes diving deeper in the blue disease while everyone lies asleep except the boy in the courtyard singing Hindi like an Orpheus, her hand reaching for the Lord of the Underworld and the throne by his side. Her journey is over and then suddenly there appears something luminous like silver filaments of a wavy coral, the glimmering fibers like the threads of life as she scoops them to the surface and unravels them on the shore. It is her death and at last she does not have to live anymore.

Then comes the doctor, a handsome man the hotel manager had called because he was afraid of cholera. "Take these pills and this package of electrolytes," says the handsome doctor, "you're dehydrated."

It tastes like lemon and she wants more of it. More water, more life with the door left open and the sun flooding her room, the courtyard full of voices and someone from the balcony yelling to the boy about the cricket match on the radio. "Hey, turn that up," the voice yells, "is England winning?" "England is losing," the boy answers.

She wants to take a bath and asks the boy to boil some water. "Who are you rooting for?" the boy asks.

She wants toast and soft-boiled eggs. She wants the mild expensive tea she bought in Darjeeling and the expensive Nagpur oranges from the south. She wants to wear a clean *kurtah* and *pajamas* and to walk outside and enjoy the rest of India.

Well again, she strolls to the *Bazaar* in the evening as if it is the ancient candystore of the east, Asia's five and dime of glittering junk and skeins of dazzling fabric, a boy squeezing sugarcane through a wringer-roller and Venus sparkling above the tents in the glowing twilight, everywhere filled with a clamor of Hindi and crazy bicycles. But what is that other sound, that tooting and bang-bang?

It comes closer, an insistent rhythm growing louder like an approaching parade. It is a parade! Where? There! And now here, suddenly louder than Sousa in a stadium it appears from the curtains like an ancient mime troupe with atavistic horns and drums, a wedding march with a solemn groom on a spangled horse in the exploding racket of his motley band, the merchants showering him with rice while he sits like a decorated puppet in a garland of marigolds and a Krishna crown, unsmiling and seeming at once both king and slave of the dancing drones who will lead him to his bride at the holy fire and she herself surrounded by maids like an egg waiting for a sperm to make more of them, more hoi polloi who will sing and starve and praise and beg as the ring of cymbals and the strains of the conch herald another shower of rice. More life! More mustaches and saris! More lepers and babies! More *sadhus* and graveyards! *Chin-chin, chini-chini,* they dance toward dawn and the lifting of the veil, the darkness opening into a protoplasmic stream of their need to live and keep singing.

She wants to join them, she wants to go home with them, but they move on and the old horse clumps away, the motley group melting into a diminuendo of the tooting and bang-bang, the *chini-chini* sinking into a peal of bicycle bells and an old man sitting quietly in their wake in a tiny stall stuffed with *beedies* and *Palmolive.*

The old man stares back like an ancient turtle with his bald head and big eyes under the bare electric bulb like an avatar of the night. Is he not that old black woman in Harlem years ago, Nisargadatta, the beedie maker who just died in Bombay, William Blake in metempsychosis or a pet turtle in a bathtub, a pair of eyes in the void like a face in the mirror after a failed suicide?

She has seen him everywhere, he is the old man of India always near as if the tourist bureau has placed him like a guide to insight and awareness. He is the old shoemaker who sewed her *Birkenstocks* at the side of a road in Aurangabad and the old wallah who pulled the rickshaw in Calcutta, he is the old attendant by the caves of Ellora while a giant Buddha sat inside like a garbage can for all the crap in her mind, he is the Buddha himself who looking at the site of his final extinction said to his friends, *"Colorful and rich, varied and resplendent, is India, and lovable and charming are the lives of her people."*

"Hello," she says, and he waves his head as if to music in the common gesture of hello and goodbye, see you in a ghetto in Oakland some day.

She passes on, her eyes panning like a camera and leaving the *bazaar* behind, the set turning into a quiet street but still the same movie with the same director, The God With The Moon In His Hair. After tracking a long brick wall she stops at some burlap bundles on a sheet of newspaper and rags, then suddenly they are moving, for they are not bundles but a family who huddle on the sidewalk with the burlap for blankets.

"Excuse me," she says. That's all right, they babble, it's a free sidewalk, come join us under the stars indifferent to the interest rate, come lie with us and enjoy the moon for tonight is paradise.

Their voices dissolve in the breeze and the quiet street leads into a park, a long angelic chant of *chay garam chay* wafting from a boy selling tea in the plaza, a fat mama and a skinny papa strolling with their two kids eating bananas, a young man with his hands behind him babbling silliness to a young woman who giggles in her palm. He wants to kiss her, he wants to fuck her, she wants romance and warmth and to feel him inside her, there is no end to their desire as it flows into the the leper begging by the bougainvillea, the stump of his body like an infant in a universe where no one wants to die, everyone body to body in a cosmic body politic, each star a life and each life a web of animals and fish, now shark, now cow, now lovely woman carrying a basket of shit on her head like a huge tiara.

Then the woman's eyes stare back like Haiti and her body coils like Somalia and Peru. Here, she seems to say, this is also India. Here, carry this basket of shit on your head and don't flatter yourself with visions, we all want a good life and it begins in the body, rejoice in our common body and starve with the rest of us.

There is nowhere else to go and nothing ahead but America. How can she return to a land without buffalo and shit always secret? Yet she is ready now to face even America. She will finally finish *The Brothers Karamazov* in the tattered *Penguin* she has carried across the continent and Dimitri will go to America and not kill himself like Ivan. She too will not kill herself and insult all the faces who want to live, the old wallahs warming their toes by a small fire or the old women selling jicamas in baskets, nor even the mosquito who bites her chin as she looks through the window of the train.

She devours their faces as if they will feed her in the great American hunger that lies ahead, all the faces like the sparrows who try to build a nest in her room as if there is no difference between inner and outer space, all the lowly clerks she follows at lunchtime to the scrapwood tables behind a garage where the tables are filled with brass pots of mashed bean and curry sauces, all the lips she wants to eat in the same way they shovel their curries with their homemade chapattis from the small tin cans.

One of them offers her a chappati and she eats it as if she can taste his life and his wife's fingers and the little home they build like sparrows with their meager wages, then she too rinses her mouths at the watertank and rubs her teeth in *namaste*.

Then comes her last night in India and when the plane is delayed she sleeps on the floor squeezed between the families as if on a steerage deck, a handkerchief around her eyes and her shoulder snug in the belly of life while the universe keeps expanding. So too does a new life begin to swell in her as if the spirit of India is giving her a child for the one she lost, a tiny larva feeding like an embryo as if her belly were its universe.

She will have India inside her more intimately than she knows and about a year from now it will emerge like an emissary from all the chay stalls and delicious picnics. There will be a concert in a church by a campus and Vilayat Khan will stroke a sitar like a phallus at the altar and then sway his head like a turtle chanting *Jingle Bells*, a river of memories flowing from his wand like words leading to words, *India, Indos, sindhu, river,* returning by music and fretting the air and *oh* the audience would sigh, *oh India,* coiling and shining like a magical worm.

Then the worm will float with her turds the next morning in her American toilet bowl, about six inches long as if it is India itself whispering, *"Here, have a round worm to remember me by, here is the other side of my music like the hole under the strings, here is my shakti with a knife in one hand and the sadhu's head in another."*

Ascaris Lunibricodes, the lab report will say, and the doctor will look it up to write a prescription. *Vermox* pills, two pills a day for three days. A bunch of dollars for the doctor

THE GREAT AMERICAN LONELINESS

and more for the druggist, enough to feed an Indian village. But there will be a warning on the label: DO NOT TAKE THESE PILLS IF YOU ARE PREGNANT OR THINK YOU ARE PREGNANT. She will not be pregnant but a mother to a worm that will crown with her shit.

She leaves India at dawn through a tunnel to the plane like a birth canal, a young ticket clerk in a neat mustache saying *at-cha* for the last time. Then the control tower rises in a clear and ruby sky while one of the groundcrew scratches his balls and stare west, the plane taxiing and waiting for a *British Airways* to take off first and a young hostess demonstrating a life preserver around her breasts while the runway appears, the sun rising as India crumbles like the Buddhas and Sivas in the monuments. Nothing is permanent, not even misery, the early light recalling the mounds of Khajuraho when she had walked there one morning with the egret and the killdear perched by the pond and the green papayas like huge testicles and the sienna bricks bevelled with shadows by the spears of the sunrise, each brick a figure with a parrot fluttering in their limbs and an old man offering marigolds to the phallus and vulva. *"Fuck for me,"* he sang, *"climb upon each other's buttocks and make more of us, more life to join the shit-eating boar and the old buffalo who turns the potted water-wheel."*

The plane rises over wrinkled hills and a river like a vein, then over the tankers in the Gulf and the bones in the desert and the ruins of Rome and the banks of Switzerland, the ice floes in the North Atlantic like stepping stones to the an empire of bombs, the old man still singing, *"I glory in the pomegranates of your breasts, I rejoice in the elephants of your loins, I exult with triumph in the silver fish of your eyes ."*

THE GREAT AMERICAN LONELINESS

PUER ETERNIS

We still play. And pray that our legs will last.
For we would be that boy again, alone in the schoolyard, his heart filled with the sky and the vision of the hoop.

The winter clouds explode with his longing, his feet numb on the frozen pavement, his hands red and swollen. Step light, sweet child, weave through the cold air and glide for your lay-up.

He practices, he practices. Driven by his legs and the dream of flying, he prays, *Please let me make it.* Not for fame, not for fortune, not even for a girl, but himself, deep in the vision of his own magnificence. There is no end to his desire, he must be perfect from every side. The clouds wait for him to reach their thunder, and he pivots, leaps, and twirls into the twilight.

He dribbles dark streets and shoots to himself through the market town. *Swish, swish,* he never misses. And comes home exhausted, ball at his side, hungry for a huge dinner to grow immense. He pores over the sports page and tapes his heroes on the bedroom wall. He adventures into the night to watch them close. They are gods in their luminous uniforms and he's in love with them. The time will come when he too will carry a duffel and wear a letter on his coat. Beautiful girls will cheer his name and he too will take his place on the great court.

It happens, the glow of the moon on the snowy walk and the flash of the bright gym. Earth odor of the locker room and his genitals snug in the jock strap. Squeak of the magic floor and the drum of balls in warm-up. His heart leaps.

And now his arms will shine and his face will flush and throb. He bobs. He shakes his hands. Will he make it? Will he float beatific through the wild chanting? *Please*, he prays, *please let me make it.* And become beautiful like the deer and the wolf and even the eagle, the innocent animal he would worship in himself, eternally hunting and hunted, body to body in the sacred dance. *Please.*

But neither struggle nor desire nor the clouds themselves can help him, and no boy escapes the inevitable wound. For he's not as good as he wants to be and someone else is always better.

He learns to hate in order to win. He can't stand to lose. He turns and punches his best friend.

The crowd is merciless and he lets go of his vision.

He falls.

He becomes a man.

And the years pass on the long journey of retreat.

Yet always beneath the scar in his eyes there lives the image of that angel who once ran to get "choosed" into the game every saturday morning, the longing to be great and the joy of pretzels and soda while he waited.

And now we are forty.

And come to the court from a troubled marriage or money problems, from the suicide of a friend and a painful failure in the mirror when we shave.

Now there is no crowd as we walk into the gym and undress. The butcher, the baker, the lawyer, the teacher, the writer, the painter, the cabinet-maker, the builder, the salesman and the therapist. Cigarette smokers, beer drinkers.

Dreamers of beautiful women and a perfect work. Praising athletes half our age.

We want him back, the boy now bald and grey who puffs and grunts up court, gluttonous for another shot. Our knees won't last forever and yet we still keep driving. Not for fame, not for fortune, but to share whatever it is that keeps us alive.

Now we need each other to make sides.

Now we apologize for bursts of rage.

And recognize each other's wound.

Dear life, we are humble in your grace and praise our breath.

Send us now to each other and the vision of the boy who once roamed a strange neighborhood in search of a hoop.

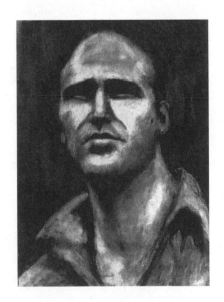

THE GREAT AMERICAN LONELINESS

THE BIG GAME

I didn't know I was the supreme reality, I thought I was a young man with a passport and a destination. When my friend, Hass, tells this story he makes me into a budding intellectual who just came from London wearing a foreign correspondent raincoat with Sartre in my pocket. The truth is I actually did have one of those long coats with all those flaps and buttons, my old friend, Bill Belli, got it from his friend, James Jones, who had worn it in Paris until he bought a new one. I loved *From Here To Eternity* in those days and I would wear the coat as if a hero's talent would rub on to me, but it was stolen in the States. Nevertheless, it was true that I still carried a lot of baggage from the old world.

I had been gone in the three years from the Free Speech Movement in '64 to the Summer of Love in '67, but I would read about them in the *Evening Standard* while waiting for my stew and *fasulah* in *Jimmy's* on Dean Street in Soho, a part of me wanting to go back and see what was happening in the land of hamburgers. In the meantime my friend, Pinsky, was at Stanford and he told me to apply for a Stegner like the one he had. He was gone when I arrived but he gave me the name of Ed McClanahan who was a friend of Ken Kesey and I told Ed how much I liked Kesey's novel, *Sometimes A Great Notion*. Then Ed called one morning to say Kesey was crashing at his place after leaving the joint and that he needed a ride to his probation officer in Redwood City because Ed had to teach that day. Sure, I said, but I had to rush because the call had awakened me and I ate only a slice of toast before I left, my empty stomach about to play a big part in the rest of the day.

Kesey was only in his early thirties then, but I was only twenty-seven and I looked up to him as an artist and a man. He was very famous at the time, which is why he got busted for grass and was jailed in a work-farm near Soledad. He was a good young man who was wise for his years and had a strong and gentle handshake, but he seemed odd at first with the free-box clothes too tight for his chunky limbs and his posture planted solid like an enormous child, especially with his shiny baldness and blond curls. Later I'd learn that innocence was indeed a part of his essential goodness and trusting nature. Looking closer at his front teeth I noticed one of them was striped red with a patch of blue. His dentist did that, he said, he lost his cap in the joint and his dentist friend dyed the new one like the flag.

I pulled the sunroof open in my old '60 Bug and he introduced me to his wife, Fay, a quiet and attractive young woman with a strong presence like his own. Where was I from? she asked. West Hoboken, I said, and they both chuckled. Why were they chuckling? McClanahan hurried the message, they said, and not getting it straight they expected a Nigerian from Armenia or an Armenian from Nigeria.

Kesey chatted about the joint and I about my work in Harlem before I went abroad, then back at McClanahan's Fay left to meet someone, so Kesey and I hung out in a cozy little rec room that was decorated with batik spreads and a huge blow-up of the Marx Brothers, Harpo smoking a hookah and popping his trademark eyeballs, his blond curls like Kesey's. Kesey was no Harpo but a part of him wanted to be, for there was a heaviness in him that he wanted to lighten and his shoulders seemed to curve under a burden he had to carry silently. Everyone carries some kind of burden and I felt his in the quiet gentleness of his powerful body that could hurt someone if he let go. I haven't seen him in twenty years and maybe I'm imagining this now, for I never got to know him well, but in person, at least with me, he was very different from his unleashed and energetic prose.

As we lounged around the rug he opened a book and started to read from it. He discovered it in the joint, he said, and it was called the *I Ching*, which I, who was still trying to read Sartre, had never heard of, so I felt strange when he asked me to throw some coins on the rug. Then the phone rang and when he returned he said it was "the Doctor," who would be over in a few minutes. Expecting a real doctor I was surprised to see a young man wearing jeans like an handsome hood who had just stolen a tank of gas. He wasn't a hood, I would learn, but just a nice young man like a favorite cousin or a familiar delivery boy. I couldn't imagine what was in the tank, but Harpo Marx and the *I Ching* and Kesey's tooth were all in progress now, and I had no wish to stop it. Though I had been around the block with some moldy cactus from *Smith's Cactus Ranch* back in the Village in '60, I had yet to learn the real meaning of what made William James write *Varieties of Religious Experience* and of the expression, *It's a gas, man.*

After Kesey and the Doctor sucked their fill they handed me the nozzle and a few minutes later the three of us were rolling around the rug hugging each other, the *I Ching* probably open to an auspicious page and Harpo's eyebrows rising higher. It was then that Kesey turned to me and said, "Cosmo, that's your name, the Armenian Cosmo." He liked to give names to his new friends as if he were a guru, and mine sounded good. Cosmo, sure, why not?

The tank was not full when we started and finishing too soon we didn't want to return to ordinary reality, so Kesey took an upper to keep the high going and gave me one too. I never liked them before but I accepted in a gesture of friendliness, and that's when Fay returned and said so and so were waiting in a car to ride up to San Francisco. Thinking it was a private trip I was about to split when Kesey asked if I wanted to come along. Okay, I said, I'd leave my Bug by McClanahan's and return when I returned. I was young and I could do whatever I wanted, right, Cosmo?

Arriving at dusk, which in mid-November was around suppertime, we parked by a little church which Kesey's friend, an Armenian lawyer if I'm not mistaken, had remodeled into a home, and Kesey said it had been an Armenian church.

The high from the gas was long gone and I was jittery from the upper which was probably some kind of diet pill, my stomach tight and empty. Inside the former church were a bunch of young folk like ourselves and I was told that some of them were from a new rock group called *The Grateful Dead*, the ominous name purling like the cigarette smoke in the empty space where the pews used to be, everyone hanging out quietly in the nacred light and waiting for the chicken that was frying in the kitchen behind the former alter.

Kesey, wanting me to feel at home, gave me another pill, then holding my shoulder he introduced me as "Cosmo" to a young woman he called "Black Maria." Though he assumed the role of a paterfamilias, he was sincere and compassionate and he wished everyone well, and wanting Maria and me to get acquainted he left us alone and joined some others. She must have been in her early twenties at the time, just a child to me now, but with her long wild hair and her mysterious silence she really did seem a Black Maria and not the innocent young Jewish girl from San Jose she really was. Too tense to talk or to eat the chicken, I saw some guys in the corner passing around a big mug, and though I figured it was more than tea I finished it thinking there would be more while the others stared at me, one of them saying, "Groovy, man."

Meanwhile someone said "The Doors" were playing in "Winterland," neither of which I had ever heard of, and Kesey called a "Bill Graham" to ask if we could all get in, all of us arriving a few minutes later in the back of a delivery truck.

As we walked in I asked the Doctor for a ride back to Palo Alto afterwards and he said sure, just meet him by the door in the lobby. Then inside the pavilion someone said let's go nearer to the stage, but the music was too loud and starting to feeling unsteady I sat alone in the last row by the door where I would meet the Doctor. I'd just sit here and observe everything, I thought, for this was my first "rock concert." Why were they called "The Doors," I wondered? Then the unsteady feeling reminded me of the peyote buds in the Village and I recognized inside my navel the same uncoiling flow like the protoplasmic swirl of tiny bubbles in the cell of an amoeba in freshman biology. The peyote trip had been mild and thinking it was happening again I decided to sit back and flow with it. I had handled it once before and I could handle it again, I thought, so I'd just sit and wait for the Doctor to meet me by the door.

Black Maria came instead. "Comon," she said, "let's join the others." "Oh no," I heard myself say, "I can't." "Why can't you?" she asked with a smile. "Because," I said, my hands gripping the seat as if I were in a plane that had lost a wing, "if I leave this seat I'll never get back to Palo Alto." "Oh sure you will," she said, still smiling. "Oh, no," I said, gripping with every muscle I could find as if I would unravel into bubbles should I ever let go, "the Doctor said he would meet me by the door and take me back to Palo Alto, I have to get back to Palo Alto." My car, my typewriter, my mirror and everything that glued me together, were all in Palo Alto, and if I left that seat I would lose them forever. "Oh, don't worry," she said, "you'll get back to Palo Alto, come with me and I'll show you the way." "You will?" I whimpered, and I was suddenly three years old again and she the great Maria who could lead me home in a sea of alien faces. "Sure, I will," she said, and letting go of my seat that was my raft I grabbed her skirt as if it were a life-line through the maelstrom of the crowd. "Are you sure?" I said, "are you sure you will show me the way?" "Sure," she said, looking over her shoulder with a Mona Lisa smile that could be lethal, "sure, I'll show you the way, and . . ." And what, where was she leading me, her voice now like a siren's and her Medusa hair electric in the strobes? "And you'll show *me* the way," she said. Oh no, I moaned, she drank that same tea, and I let go of her and fell to the floor while the lead singer, Jim Morrison, bellowed like an echo through the mews of an endless labyrinth. *"Show me the way. . . ."* he sang. Yes, I moaned, show me the way, show me the way! *"To the next whiskey bar,"* he sang next. Oh no, I cried, I would never get back to Palo Alto, I would be unravelled like a Cosmo endlessly lost, and it was there on the floor of a former ice rink that this *I* who is typing these words first encountered what could never be written and where we can't hold on any longer or have any reason to hold on. There was something in the tea much stronger than a few cactus buds, especially, I would learn, since it was pure Owsley acid, and with a dexedrine in an empty stomach it was more than enough to open the doors of my perception.

The ecstasy did not last of course, and then this *I* appeared again, and with it the deep crying that was somehow entwined with grief and guilt like a purgatory, then the crying was over and I opened my eyes and that's when the hell began, Morrison singing *"Light My Fire"* as I struggled to get back to Palo Alto and the Peter I had been there, the more I panicked the more I suffered like a lost child terrified of the darkness, the harder I held on to Peter the more intensely I was pulled away as if thrashing in an undertow. Then suddenly a ghost was saying hello to me. "Pete!" she said, "what are you doing here?"

It was Marjorie Katcher. Marjorie Katcher was Belli's old girlfriend back in New Brunswick, in fact I introduced them when she was in Douglas and I in Rutgers and so on and so forth like hermetic heiroglyphs on a Dead Sea scroll. I had lost touch with her and now with a face more light than flesh she was looking at me and saying, "I'm not the Marjorie you once knew, Pete." "You're not?" I said, believing her more than she could know. "Oh no," she said, "the Marjorie you knew is dead." "She is?" I said, not doubting her at all. "Yes," she said, "I'm reborn now." "That's good," I said, "how did you do it?" "I'm a mother now," she said, "I have a baby daughter." "Oh," I said in despair, "I can't do that." "No," she said, "you can't." "No, I can't," I said, and unable to talk with any logic I wandered off and left her on the other side of the universe.

Somehow I got back to the door in the lobby, but it was useless to me now, and who was that walking in from the street but someone I once knew back in Palo Alto, though he was now wearing a *Captain Marvel* suit. "Hey, Pete!" he said, "good to see you here!" It was Ed McClanahan, but not really. The Ed McClanahan I once knew was a jeans and flannel young professor with a wife and kids and a warm solid home, not a flashing Captain Marvel in a lobby full of freaks. Oh no, I moaned, I would never get back to Palo Alto.

"What's the matter?" he asked, "are you all right?" "No," I said, "I have to find a police station, I have to get to a hospital." I had to be Peter again, without Peter the horror would crush me into a nothingness from which I could never return, and I started to wander outside like a street person who is mentally disturbed. "Wait a minute, Pete," he said, "you don't want to go to the Police, man, that's the last place you want to go."

He had driven up to the city to join the fun, but when he saw me he gave it up to drive me back to Palo Alto, as no police or hospital could ever do. "Are you really Ed McClanahan?" I kept asking him as he drove across the freeway in his Captain Marvel suit.

Back in his rec room Harpo Marx was still sucking his hookah, but he too was different now and would remain so until I was Peter again.

"Don't worry," Ed kept saying, "in a little while you'll be Peter again and tomorrow will be the Big Game." "The Big Game? What Big Game?" "The Big Game, you know what the Big Game is, don't you?" "Sure, I know what the Big Game is, but do *you* know what the Big Game is?" "No, Pete, I don't mean that Big Game, I mean the Big Game between Stanford and Cal." "Oh, they play the Big Game too?"

And so on until the rising sun dissolved the dawn and everywhere become solid again like Daphne in a tree. Exhausted, I drove back to my flat in Menlo Park, and in the days following I felt like Helen Keller after she spelled water by touching it. "I left the well-house eager to learn," she wrote, "and every object which I touched seemed to quiver with life. That was because I saw everything with a strange new sight that had come to me."

A couple of weeks later I drove up to Kesey's farm in Oregon for Thanksgiving. He too had just seen it for the first time, since his family moved in while he was in the joint. There were other families and friends as well and they were all trying to live together, the farm and their lives in a simple beauty not at all like what would be described in a popular book, *The Electric Kool Aid Acid Test*, for everywhere was instead in rich greens and earth colors like a vision to a

city boy who grew up with streetlights. Ken Babs and the others had just built a communal dining hall and the fresh fir smelled delicious, the long dining table covered with a resin that preserved in its amber the photos from when they roamed the country in their Magic Bus full of youth and hope. Maria was there and she was now just another girl on a farm who wanted to make yoghurt and have kids. The big bathroom was at the side of the barn and when I walked in a longhair was sitting on the bowl and a young woman was taking a shower. I had not known such bathrooms in London or the Village, yet in my own childhood the bathroom door was always open and I didn't learn it was supposed to be closed until I first went to someone else's home. It was the tea full of stars that led the way to communal bathrooms, it helped show that everyone's crap was alike and no one had to be ashamed of it.

Then Neil Cassady came with a few other folk. He was in very bad shape and he would die a while later. He was coming down from a lot of speed and he looked old and sick. If he were Kerouac's age he was about twenty years older than I, or around forty seven, my age now. He stood bobbing and mumbling a bunch of monotony and I would have ignored him were he someone else, yet I felt a kind of sympathy for where he came from, as if he once fought with the Old Guard. He seemed one of the big guys in that schoolyard that had become my hunting ground after I left my mother's kitchen for the wilderness of America, he too had once been a young rebel who couldn't live in it without searching for a way out or wherever, and here he was now mumbling nonsense and very close to death. If he had ever drunk any tea full of stars it didn't lead him to yoga or landscape painting, and it was one thing to see heaven in a flower and a world in a grain of sand, but another to survive afterwards.

A couple of months later Richard Brautigan gave a reading at Stanford and my friend Gatz and I gave him a ride to San Francisco on our way home to Bolinas, where Gatz had found me a cabin near his and McGuane's.

Liking Richard I visited him in his apartment one day. He was not yet famous and it was a poor writer's apartment, bare but tidy, and though he had girlfriends he lived there alone. "Every once in a while it depresses me," he said, "and then I paint it and it feels like home again."

His voice was soft and gentle and his shoulders curved as if he were holding something in his heart that would fall away if he pulled them back. He was Kesey's age but they were very different, for Richard was very shy yet not at all good at hiding, and his sweetness was naked. Sure, he was sick with selfhood like the rest of us, but he was a generous and sensitive soul, as most good artists are, and though I would never get to know him well, I hung out with him a little after he moved near Gatz in Livingston, Montana before it too became gentrified.

"You want some lambchop?" he asked me that first time I dropped by. He had just fried some lambchops after writing all day and he was very hungry. He loved to write and though his writing was bare and tidy like his apartment, it was, when he was at his best, far out and deep, and I was surprised when Gatz told me he never had any acid or grass or anything but booze. He just tuned in with his own special antennae and was able to transmit his wonderful music which was, beneath his humor, so fresh and delicate like himself. There were other sides of him, of course, we all have our other sides, but when he was in the spirit of what he loved he was able to go through a door of a very special place and then share it without any photos in magazines or interviews. I first met him in the days of the free-box and the Diggers dishing free food in the Panhandle and he stood in his big hat and Nietzche mustache handing out free packets of flower seeds with his poems printed on one side and on the other a label, *Plant This Poem.* Not as a gim-

mick but more sincerely than maybe even he himself realized, for he really wanted to believe it was possible, he really
wanted his work to plant him in the common earth he felt
he had lost, or am I writing about myself now, yet what difference does it make?

Then he got famous around the time the flowers were
trampled in People's Park and the refugees from the mur-
derous suburbs started to camp there. America had caught
up with him and he could buy as much bourbon as he
wanted. He was drinking hard by the time he moved to
Paradise Valley, and when I visited him one afternoon I
noticed the kitchen clock was full of bullet holes like a scene
in one of his books. Paradise Valley was one of the most
beautiful I had seen and his typewriter was by a big window
looking out to a great landscape with the Absaroka in the
background, and there he sat every day though the words
didn't come as they did in the little room on Geary Street.
He owned the spread in Montana and a house in Bolinas
and a studio in North Beach, but he still kept that little
Geary Street apartment. "I don't want to lose touch with it,"
he said, "it's a part of me I don't want to lose touch with."

He died of "the Great American Loneliness," someone
said after his suicide, perhaps quoting Kerouac, or maybe
Fitzgerald? As I re-read *Trout Fishing* now its darkness feels
stronger and thus its light as well, the winos and the poor
kids like Richard himself in the nightmare of his history
and the magic of his vision pulling him through. Like the
Kool-Aid wino illuminating himself without sugar, he survived with faith and courage the hell I knew in Winterland,
at least while he could still keep writing, his love of making
lines leading him through the manic crowd until he could
face the dawn again. Then came the time, I guess, when
there was no Ed McClanahan to sit up with him, and he
couldn't do it alone anymore.

I just returned from a walk in the hills. How beautifully
they glowed around the canyon in the magical hour before

sundown, like quiet buffalos tufted with evergreen and mottled with sagebrush, the trail ablaze with college girls jogging in shorts. I climbed to the top of them and gazed across the bay as the sun sank between the pylons of the Gate, then I heard music rising from the stadium below, and it was the band practicing for the Big Game tomorrow. Then the sun fell behind the ruby and copper clouds above the Farallons and the Marin hills reclined into the bay like a great serpent, the percussion and brass echoing up the redwood grove while in the distance the freeway moaned like a prayer wheel and the city spread below like a cancer. Rising and sinking with my breath I entered my navel and imagined what the scene would look like had I drunk a mug of visionary tea, the clouds like the breathing of the sea and the cables of the bridge like a smile of Eden, the city of St. Francis a castle across the waves and Alcatraz Island a prisoner escaping through the Gate, not as metaphor but in flesh and blood that pulsed and streamed like an eternal amoeba and a leaf of grass, all those kids driving down to Palo Alto tomorrow with the Grateful Dead in their cassette decks.

THE GREAT AMERICAN LONELINESS

THE GIRL I

He entered by a bridge to a quiet lane of old brick homes with flowers on the windowsills, the gulls angelic in a violet sky and the willows graceful over the canal. Then the first one appeared, palming her breasts behind the glass as if they were her loaves of fulfillment. Come, she smiled, but the hunt was on and he had to keep moving. As if he himself were the favored prey, he had to be exhausted before he was devoured.

Feed yourself on joy, the Buddha had said, but he was so hungry he could hardly swallow, their rooms like stalls in the night of a Feast and he a child who wanted them all, each a treasure in a frame in the rainbow glimmer of the porno shops.

Tumid and throbbing he rested by the ruins where the canal curved and the red lights disappeared, his genitals quieted by the glowing moss and the fugitive hues of the sundown. He could have sat by the canal and the hunger would have dissolved in the changing light, but needing to piss he returned to the urinal by the *Oude Kirk* and the little bridge full of junkies.

A man was masturbating staring through the grill at the whore by the church, his eyes lowered when he left, as if from a confession booth.

In the stall his piss wet the man's tissue as he looked through the grill himself, the whore still there. The church was now a monument and across the polished pavement she stood by her door like a middleaged housewife, her chubby cheeks haloed by her bleached hair.

Outside the urinal a family of tourists were strolling by for their after-dinner entertainment. "Get a look at this one, Melvin," said the woman with an American accent, her hair bleached like the whore's. They were the same age and seemed the eternal whore and housewife with an eternal Melvin in between.

The whore ignored them and smiled at him instead, but he turned into a narrow alley where Mrs. Melvin wouldn't point her finger when he made his choice.

Yet how was he to choose when they were like the bread in his dreams in so many forms and sizes? They posed behind their windows like wonders to a boy on a Saint's night, his fingers gripping tight to his only nickel until he found the right one. Here they were each waiting to fulfill him and all he needed was a yes.

But how bad they could be if he were wrong, their

flesh like a tissue in a pissing stall by an empty church, all the refugees from humanity's toilet and its famines and wars, his own hunger fused with shame. No, not this one nor that, their faces like photos from a history of pain.

The narrow alley seemed a crack to an underworld and the men squeezed by like spectres, then amid the beckoning smiles a young woman stood in the rear of her room as if for those beguiled by the distant kind. Yes, he was one of them and he almost stopped as if he had found her.

Afraid to commit himself he walked further into the alley and a few doors later there was another one more glamorous, but again he couldn't stop and came out of the alley like a boy still holding his nickel.

Exhausted and desperate he needed to piss again, and he smoked another cigarette, one more cigarette to smother his hunger among the ogling tourists and the junkies by the bridge.

Enough pain, he decided to return to the glamorous one, and he hurried as if she might disappear, yet when he came to her window the curtain was drawn and he would not wait to follow someone else. The hunt was over. As if he himself were being chosen he arrived by the one in the back of her room, and she nodded as if she knew he would return.

"Would you like to come in?" she said in English, her slight accent congenial and erotic.

He entered as if into another realm, the small room in warm pinks like the labia of a conch. She was young enough to be his daughter, but she guided him as if he were blind in this world where she were queen.

Watching her undress he trembled as he stepped from his pants and folded them on the chair. Would he be hard enough, he who had always needed to prove himself by staying hard? "I may have some trouble," he said, as if asking for help.

"Yes?" she said, and like a gentle nurse she washed his penis in the sink. *Don't worry,* she seemed to say, *you're in good hands, I'm a good whore, this is what you pay me for.*

Fifty guilders, twenty-five dollars. For a moment he longed for all his life.

She gestured for him to lie on the bed and then lay over him and rubbed her mound on his penis, the glow of her flesh like the surge in his loins as he let go of all worrying. Now hard enough and confident, he sighed with relief that he had found her at last. "You like it?" she asked, pleased that she was pleasing him and he wanting to please her too. "Yes," he said, "I like it very much."

Before he knew it the condom was on and she slipped him inside, then she began riding him with his hands reaching up to palm her breasts, his fingers tipping her nipples in counterpoint to the slow bobbing of her buttocks, his eyes looking up at her rising from his loins as if she were a cathedral who would lift him into the arches of her pleasure, it was her pleasure that untied his knots and he felt himself rising and wanting to go higher, her warmth unravelling what he could never release alone and her lips open as if in a welcome home, the channels unlocking for a light to flow through. How long they had been closed, how far he had journeyed for the key. "Let me get on top," he said. "You want to get on top?" she said. "Yes," he said, on top of her as in the flying in his dreams.

Turning in their embrace his penis softened and slipped out, then she slipped it in again and he wanted to go further like a light that could flow to her eyes and into his own. Stretching in a cobra pose he stared entranced at her sighing while their genitals lay together like animals in a lair. For a rare and blissful moment he felt they were somehow married and his longing was gratified inside her.

He could pump now without holding back, the condom and the years like a dike for coming too soon. Nor did he need to wait for her who would be there to meet him. She didn't whisper his name, she didn't even know his name, yet she caressed his spine as if she had known him all his life, and he held her with gratitude and love. She could feel that he was loving her, and having reached her oasis he was pumping for a life in her embrace. She herself would open as much as she could, though not all the way of course, it was understood that she could open only part of the way, then he would be on his own where she could not follow. Pausing to thank her, he touched her tenderly around her eyes and she raised her buttocks to let him plunge even deeper.

It was time, the channels had opened until there was only the last to be unlocked, all of him pumping to find that place where all boundaries would dissolve and her flesh would be as familiar as his own. *O come with me*, he wanted to whisper, *here inside us, my dearest wife, O life, I want you inside me*, and it seemed as if she understood, for she was now pumping with him until there came the flowing and the overflowing and his eyes in her hair as she caressed his spine, an old bird gliding to her glen and folding his wings in her quiet limbs, soft and detumescent and calm and quaffed, large and powerful and unbound and free.

"Let me lie here for a moment," he said. "Yes," she said, "of course."

Where was he now? He lay with his face in her hair as if he were washed upon an island with a jungle by the shore. He didn't want to leave. He wanted to stay in the jungle of her odor and the warmth of her moistness. Why did he have to leave, why?

She moved gently and his time was up. No more jungle, no more island, the sea of this world like a rising tide that would swallow him once again.

He sat on the bed while she washed her vulva with a small towel, their intimacy lingering as he gazed at her naked for one last time, his eyes desperate to etch her in memory before she disappeared. He studied her buttocks and the way she held the towel between her thighs, her neck curving into the muscles of her shoulder and her hair flowing like an after-image he could never touch, her beauty receding and becoming even more intense.

She looked at the silkscreen on his old T-shirt, a dolphin leaping in the air. "Are you from America?" she said. "Yes," he said, "were you ever there?" "No," she said, "it's too expensive."

It was over. They were back in the world of money and time, her face and voice now mortal and particular. Who was she now who had been a queen and how could he take her to America like a dolphin from the other realm?

She looked at him as if reading his thought, and she smiled as if to say it was all right, he could have her anytime he wanted and she would never say no, as long as he could pay.

How much, how much would it cost to pull her from this underworld and have every day, what was her own hunger? "What is your name?" he said. "Tanya," she said. "Is that your real name?" he said. She smiled as if to say what difference did it make?

"What is your name?" she said. "Peter," he said. "Is that your real name?" she said, still smiling. "I don't know, he said, "that's what my father named me." "It's a nice name," she said, "but I will call you Piet, is it all right if I call you Piet?"

He loved her. He had loved her even before she was born and he wanted to marry her as if she could lead him home again, the fifty guilders lying by the mirror where she had left them when he first came in. "Thank you," he said, and he looked into her eyes as deeply as he could. She looked back and saw how much he meant it. "Thank *you*," she said, as if for more than the money.

Stepping into the lane he peered over his shoulder and she nodded farewell like the end of movie.

It was night now, and he walked like a child still half-asleep with a happy dream, the sky still glowing in the solstice and a gibbous moon rising above the rooftops. Quiet and calm, he did not need to piss or smoke or make any more decisions, he did not have any need at all, and as he stepped from the alley he looked up to read the name of the lane on the corner house. *Trompetter's Steed*, it said, the white letters on the blue enamel like somewhere in a children's book, The Little Alley Where The Queen Lives.

He walked along the canal and found a bench by a willow tree, a gull gliding like a holy ghost in a pearl blue sky, the moon not a skull but a chubby face with a smile, then looking over his shoulder he saw another whore reclining behind her window while the tourists passed her as if in a zoo.

He stared at the water as if it could reconcile her misery with his peace, somehow misery had to be transformed into love, somehow the loss of love had to be transformed into love itself. Look, said the water, look at the whore and the tourists and the geraniums on the windowsill, let peace lead to awareness.

The gull glided around the moon and all would be well as long as he had fifty guilders, peace and fulfillment for the price of Tanya and no need for cigarettes to smother the pain, no more masturbating by churches and no more junkies on a bridge, no more Mrs. Melvin with a pointy finger and no more girls in cages, just peace and fulfillment with a Queen. He walked to Rembrandt Square and as he waited for the tram he undressed everyone with how naked he felt.

Back in his room he fell asleep thinking of when he could see Tanya again, then in a dream he fled through a ghetto from enemies who wanted to kill him, and in another dream a woman went away and left him alone.

In the morning there was another war and famine in the news and another psychotic had killed a child.

He shaved with the window open and the weather glorious, the ducks flowing in the canal as if in a fairyland. How to make them one, the glowing ducks and the bloody

slaughter in his huge and historic nose? Who was the face in the mirror who was never good enough for joy? He was *The One Who Did Not Know Himself*, the creature who lived alone. Once upon a time life nurtured him for forty-seven years and none of them said why. Why was he not one of those who died in the headlines every morning? If you want to paint a portrait, said the mirror, you must see the skull beneath the flesh, if you want to paint the light you must surround it with darkness.

Through the window of the train the fields unravelled under billowing cumulus like the Ruysdaels of his youth, the passing windmills sprouting a cinema of memories through the flashing glass. Here now Holland and yet it could have been India or the Great Plains, that farmgirl with daffodils the one who sold jicama in Aurangabad or the waitress in Wisconsin, the brick homes in double exposure with the Americans who chatted across the aisle.

"Should we get off at Leyden?" the mom asked her family. She was worried it was the wrong train and they should switch at Leyden.

He knew who she was. She was little Mildred with silken hair her mother braided every morning and tied with rubber bands. She had disappeared after fifth grade and did not die, she did not starve to death in Cambodia or rip to pieces from a rocket in Beirut. Here she was now wearing clothes and a haircut, her vulva familiar from Tanya the night before, the sister human he never married. *Why not, O, Mildred, why not?*

She filed her nails and chewed her cheek while the dad and the kids talked about the good time they were going to have. She had a home with them in a place called *Happiness* and he knew her as if he once lived there. Those shoes she was wearing, so stylish yet comfortable, she bought them one saturday before shopping in the market by the square, he had stood behind her by a stall and watched her caress an aubergine and pinch a zucchini at the tip, she was the woman of purple and green and he had painted her since he first discovered she was not himself.

The clouds curled into her ears and the train rocked along the canal between her thighs, her knees stiff like the skeleton in his closet brought to life. He had studied her anatomy all his life and yet she never came out right, the little Mildred who had lived behind a door and then disappeared, she always disappeared.

She sat across the memories as if posing for his biography, the little Mildred who became Silvana who wrote her name in his notebooks and then went out with someone else, her beauty the lips he never kissed until they were seniors and he reached up from below her step as if she were the end to all his pain, her lips easing away and never kissing him again.

She didn't want to be the end to anyone's pain, she wanted to be a mother and a wife and here she was a mother and a wife who was once Celine in college he wanted so deeply she slept with him with her clothes on, her powerful hair and hypnotic buttocks like the great eunuch of her virginity. Three years he longed to fuck her and for three years she danced around him with a fever of her own, each of them with a different fever in a world where they would dance alone.

She crossed her legs and touched her earlobe while the light played on the phases of her life, the little Mildred so vitally bright and the young Silvana so cheerful and vivacious, the passionate Celine he could never see clearly as if all the colors in the colorwheel had converged into mud. Here now he had to be free of her who had become the painful Jewel who had stabbed his eyes with the knife above his bed, the angry Jewel like the final cast of a mold he had been forming all his life, the sweet Jewel who had opened her thighs and whispered in his cheek, "O, *it feels so good, it feels so good.*"

She reached in her bag for a book and then buried the title in her crotch. He knew what it was about, it was a book a Jewel would read, it was a woman's book, a foreign novel about a war of silence and a battlefield of loneliness, it was about waking at four in the morning and reaching for a coronary to end it all.

He turned to her and spoke across the aisle as if it were the void between their lives. "It's the right train," he said, I'm also going to The Hague." "Thank you," she said, and pulling her skirt over her knees she continued reading, the wrinkles around her lips like the scars of a tombstone, the flower that was once her smile now the dried apple of all the years she never answered his letters.

He turned and stared at the swift clouds and their dark patterns across the sunny landscape, his love for her severed by the memory of her door. *Do you think*, she had said, holding the lock, *that just because you put your cock inside me it means I love you?*

In the park by the Mauritshaus he ate his bread and cheese on a bench under a plane tree. How bountiful life had been with all the bread and cheese across the continents, all the chapattis and lavash across the broken stones and all the tortillas and loaves by the cobbles and the ruins, Greenpeace picketing the World Court nearby.

He sat like a king overlooking his treasures, the bajia and samosas by the broken Buddhas in Ellora and the cucumbers and pretzels by the neglected Saint Sophia, the pastry and coffee by the broken Parthenon and the *pain de compagne* by the void in Arles where the war had bombed Van Gogh's yellow house.

Here now at another shrine, he feasted on the wonder of food and how it came from a seed of grass and a stone, so many seeds crushed and kneaded with the water of life. He chewed and swallowed as if in communion, he ate his apple and drank his water and thanked whatever it was that made them possible, something to do with civilization and the museums of a pilgrimage, the great orphanage that kept him alive and all he had to do was cure himself.

He walked inside.

It was another museum built with money from a slave trade, a pleasant cafe downstairs by the restrooms. He had come for the Vermeer and the Rembrandt but there was a good De Hooch and a Rubens as well. First he would piss and have a cup of coffee for dessert.

He had a table to himself with a vase of some purple what were they called and some tiny white and yellow something like daisies, a lovely young waitress wiping it clean while he studied her breasts and how she moved in her blue skirt and maroon-striped jacket, her hair falling softly over her eye. *How wonderful it was,* he wrote in his journal, *to fuck Tanya last night.* The young waitress smiled and moved to the other tables, his pen charged with her buttocks and the power of caffeine.

He sat as if he were the Governor himself in his mansion of art, the ghosts of slaves in the marble. He turned and looked over his shoulder at the large painting of a slaughtered rabbit on a table of a feast. *Dear Death*, he wrote, *I love to write.*

He was now ready to climb the stairs.

He climbed the stairs. He climbed as if he were in a church where a boy went to pray by the candles while an old priest dozed in a throne and the incense wafted from a thurible, a nickel clinking in the brass and the silence of the flames, the horror of religion like a dragon behind the altar. He climbed as if into his sickness itself and the dark adytum of something feminine, he climbed like a cripple who wanted to win her with a light, he climbed to see her as he had climbed to the caves of Elephanta and the height of the Parthenon, the vagina of Notre Dame and the mounds of Khajuraho, he climbed into his life of art and all the years he was her monk who wanted to see her naked, he climbed to see her for whom like the monks of Cybele he had swung from a cliff with an iron hook in the muscles of his back. *"Ah, art,"* Degas once said after singing an aria while the model waited, *"you bitch."*

She was in the little room to the left of the stairs and some people were whispering in Dutch. Here she was in the original who had stared at him in his bedroom when he woke, the old print fading like an image of a lost girl in another realm. They were all like that really, all the prints and postcards like a lost family in a desert, the faces of grandparents and uncles he never embraced. Here she was now whom no forger nor memory could repeat, the girl of his dream who embraced him into radiance and disappeared when he woke, his day becoming night.

The others left the room and she was so alone a maniac could have slashed her face and ripped her bodice into shreds. He could be the maniac who had shot Leonardo's Anne in the breast or the one who burned Rembrandt's Danae with kerosene. *Let me in*, he would yell, *you in the radiance behind the window I can never penetrate. Noli me tangere*, she would answer, *I am the girl in the distance you can never approach, I am the pearl beyond reach.*

She looked over her shoulder like an epiphany. That was what art was about, something to do with the way she said, *You see me now but I'll be gone when you leave.*

He didn't want to leave. He wanted to paint her in himself so he would never need her again. Millimeter by millimeter he crawled through the crackled pigment as if he were Vermeer himself placing her in

space, the path from her bodice to her turban like the centuries from Leonardo to Phidias to whoever they were always making lines.

Century by century he crawled across her figure as if he were the apprentice who ground the stones for each tone and shade, the weaver of the linen and the gleaner of the linseed, the slaughtered rabbit of the glue and the sable of the brush. Stroke by stroke he modeled her flesh as if to caress the curve of her neck and all who died to make her live, her lips parting as if they were his hunger to kiss them. How old was she, or was she even mortal? She glowed like the dawn the sun would turn to a laurel, *The Girl With The Pearl Earring* by a Vermeer who died poor.

He walked around the room with her eyes following him. He would never see her again. He would leave that room and she would still be there after he died. He would leave the universe and she would still be parting her lips with *The Secret Beyond Revealing*.

He left to see the Rembrandts before closing time. The Self-Portrait, the last one, was on the other side of the stairs, the girl now a bulbous nose and a crusty jowl, the cheek and nostril glazed like a quiet battlefield, the crimsons and violets like shit and blood.

You called us art, they said, *but we are no religion or hero-worship, and even spirit would be wrong. We are an old man in an empty house and all our children are dead. We are the addiction and the line you never got right. We are the years in a room while a squirrel waved her tail on the fence and you wouldn't answer the knock on the door. We are the junkies on the other side of the wall and the whore down the hall by the cockroach toilet, the little Hermes on a fruitcrate and the peanut butter on the windowsill. We are all the peanut butter of unemployment and the lines of a hermit crab when the tide is low, lines upon lines washed away by your failure, take your look and go, you miserable loser.*

The guard pointed to his watch and the show was over.

On the night before his plane he planned to see Tanya as he shaved before breakfast. But woe is man who plans for getting laid. Woe is that boy shaving for the big date when the girl's mother calls and says she can't make it. She couldn't make it, she couldn't come, she wasn't there. Yet he would plan again for the rest of his years as if one day he would not have to wait anymore. He would grow up and go to college and win her with a job. He would be an artist and win her with fellowships. He would be a man, He would win. He would spend the afternoon in the Riksmuseum and then after a delicious meal he would stroll into fairyland for one last night with the beautiful Queen.

But the moon made other plans and a vulture swirled in the clouds of the weather map. Learn to flow, said the ducks in the canal as the sky turned grey, let the day decide how you'll live tonight.

No, he said, *I want! I want!* And he rushed through the galleries to stuff his eyes before the final bell, the hours too short for the vast kingdom between the *Keukemaid* and the *Siva in the Flames.*

Prowling the walls for one last look, he came in the final minutes to Rubens' starving prisoner in *Cimon And Pero,* the old hands chained to a wall and the old lips desperate for the daughter's nipple.

THE GREAT AMERICAN LONELINESS

Outside the full moon was about to rise and the workers rushed under the grey clouds. Tired and hungry he made the mistake of trying to save money with a cup of potatoes instead of staying dry in a restaurant. He searched for a cafe to escape the drizzle but when he found one it had already stopped. He worried he would be too tired to fuck.

I must rest, I thought, *so I can enjoy Tanya.* But the same forces that woke him in the dark night of the soul now joined the moon to push him there again. A cold wind swept across the canals and he caught a chill under his damp shirt. *Be there, Tanya*, he whispered to the canal, *let me know your glow again.*

She wasn't there when he came to her door. Someone else was there instead and he didn't want her, he wanted his Tanya. Exhausted and shivering he wandered without desire or erection and the fairyland now a nightmare with the whores like harpies in the neon light. It was not fucking he needed but his eyes in her hair and his arms in her embrace. Where was she who would hold him before he died? Then his legs gave out and he chose one blindly as if a deadline had passed.

She seemed at first as if he would be spared, but as soon as she took his money he realized she was not only unlike Tanya but her very opposite. She was not a gentle nurse in a sea world, she was a business woman who would use her body like a tool she would polish and sharpen, a magazine body more firm than Tanya's and of a world where even dolphins must perform. Here was the career woman who would hear no excuses from a loser who could not get hard by himself, and with her perfect breasts and firm thighs she spoke like an expensive surgeon to whom he had brought his sickness for a cure. "If you want me to blow you," she said, "it will be another fifty guilders."

He was still cold and his limbs ached and he wanted to lie down and be touched. He had tried as hard as he could, he had forced himself from bed every morning and he meditated every day and read the right books and fed the cats and sent checks to Greenpeace and World Wildlife, yet faced with the impossible task of getting hard he said, "All right then, let's forget about the fucking."

She shrugged indifference and gestured for him to lie on the bed as if he had come to have teeth cleaned, his body reclining as if he were hoping for a gas to make him feel good. He wanted to feel good, he wanted her to suck his penis as if it were the fruit of life whose juice would ooze into her mouth.

But it was not the fruit of life or anything but fifty guilders, and she sucked it fast with the condom on as if it were a snake wound she had to clean as quickly as she could.

He came without coming and something dribbled out of him bitter and rancid, his body on her bed as if in a morgue and his shame uncovered like his lungs black from all his cigarettes of despair, his evolution devolved to a disgusting worm.

"Did you enjoy that?" she asked.

Was he hearing right? Did she actually ask that? She was innocent. She had her own misery and her own reasons for why she was here. She was a poor girl who had become a whore and yet she still needed to be good. Be a good girl, said her mirror, don't lose face. Folding his money with a neat crease, she needed to know she had earned it.

He dressed while she slipped into her robe and combed her hair, each of them wearing their armor to face the world that was never home. "No," he said, "I didn't enjoy that at all."

She straightened the bed as if she didn't hear him. When he left by the stairs she said, "Will you close the door behind you when you leave?"

He left it open and staggered into the lane like an amputee. A door had been closed too many times, but instead of tearing it off he turned away and wanted to dic. The plane would leave in the morning and he would have to keep moving. Something kept him alive but he didn't want it anymore. Others craved it fiercely and struggled to the end, but he wanted to lie in the pavement like a dying animal.

He lit a cigarette and smothered his lungs with the memories of the dead, of Richard and Bernie killing them-selves and Dolly dying of cancer, of Daniel trying it with a razor and a schizophrenic in a subway one night when a crowd recoiled from his odor and his filth. What creature could stink so foul as a human being who had lost his pearl? *Dear Girl*, he whispered, *where are you, where are you?*

THE GREAT AMERICAN LONELINESS

THE GIRL II

Then came the Fulbright, again through friends. Gorbachev's *glasnost* had opened the door to Soviet Armenia and Dickran Kyoumjian prodded him to apply, Dickran and Geoffry Goshgarian and Levon Chorbajian then writing references.

In Yerevan he lived in a dorm in the center of town around the corner from the art institute. With little to do at the university, he walked to the Institute and painted the model with his new friends, young Gago Kazanjian and Khatchig what was his last name and the rest of their gang.

"I hope you find a wife," his mother had said before he left. Everyone said he would find one easily, since so many single women would jump at a chance to go to America.

But he searched in the same way as he had all his life and he found instead a whore through the nightclerk who had gone to school with her. Her name was Sirpuhi and she was only twenty-three and she had just started the trade. She had gone to college in Rostov, but she had recently quit after her father died and she earned only sixty rubles a month as a clerk. He gave her that much for an hour in the dorm.

"Don't you have any *dole-lars*," she would ask. No one told him before he came that his traveller's checks would be worthless in the Soviet Union, so all he had was the four hundred rubles from the university each month. Had he brought dollars he would have been rich and she would have stayed with him, but she would be gone by spring.

Nor would she come as often as he wanted because of the bad phones and the curfews, and when she did come she would always be late and he would look at the clock and smoke Bulgarian cigarettes. Then there would be a knock on the door and he would pour her some vodka and she would laugh at his poor Armenian. How lovely was her youth and how old he felt, how delicious her labia while she sucked his penis and how relieved he was to make her come this way, how deeply he could fuck her afterwards and how he enjoyed lying with her in the lamplight while the Chinese physicist played the accordion across the hall, a cockroach wandering over the parquet floor.

"Will you marry me and take me to America?" she said one night.

"No," he said.

"Why not?"

"Because I'm hoping I will find someone who will stay with me."

"If you haven't found someone by now it means you don't want to."

"Maybe you're right, but I still keep hoping."

"Well, keep me in mind anyway. I won't leave you right away. I'll stay with you a little and we can have a good time together."

"*Mee keech,*" he said, the Armenian words for "a little."

"Yes, a little. It would be better than nothing."

"Maybe it would be better than nothing, but I need everything now."

"Well, if you change your mind you know where I am."

"Where are you? You're here today and gone tomorrow."

"You're right, I am a restless soul, aren't I?"

She was born in that year when he was in London after Annie went to the States.

"You're a lot like a woman I once knew in London," he said.

"Was she Armenian?"

"No, she was English."

"Why didn't you marry her?"

"We were restless souls, just like you."

"Was she a whore?"

"No, she lived with another man."

"Then why did she sleep with you?"

"She liked us both."

"What happened to her?"

"She went to America."

"I want to go to America too."

"What would you do there?"

"I would buy clothes."

"She loved to buy clothes, too. She would shop in a street called Carnaby Street and it became famous for clothes."

"I love clothes."

"I know."

"Will you send me some when you go back to America?"

"I will, if you're still here."

"Where am I going? I'm stuck here."

"Don't say that. You're not stuck anywhere. You're young and you're healthy. Only the sick and the old are stuck somewhere."

"I want to get out of here. This is no country to live in."

"Because of the poverty?"

"Yes, because of the poverty."

"I wish I could help you."

"Then take me to America."

"No, I can't take you to America. I'm sorry."

She stared sadly at the ceiling as if it were the void.

"There is a boy I know who wants to marry me and take me to America."

"Well, then, there you are. Why do you sound so sad?"

"I can't marry him."

"Why not?"

"I can't kiss him. He tries to kiss me and I have to turn away. How can I marry someone I can't kiss?"

"Why can't you kiss him?"

"I just can't. He's a nice boy, but I just can't kiss him."

"How would he take you to America?"

"He has an uncle there. He wants me to go with him."

"Can't you go with him and then get divorced?"

"No, he's a good boy. I can't do that to him."

"Maybe if you stay with him a while the kissing will be all right."

"No, it will never be all right."

"You kiss me and I'm old and ugly."

"You're not old and ugly. I like kissing you."

"Maybe after you stay with him a kind of love will grow between you."

"How am I going to stay with him when I can't kiss him? Kissing is the most important thing between a man and woman."

"The eskimos kiss with their noses. Maybe you can kiss with your noses."

"Oh you, there you go with your nose again. I'm serious."

"I know you are."

"I want to go to America."

"America will come here someday and you will have all the clothes you want."

"I will be old by then."

"Maybe not. Maybe it will be sooner than you think."

"I put my brassiere on backwards this morning."

"What does that mean?"

"It means I will have bad luck."

"No, it doesn't. Don't think about it and it won't mean anything."

They lay in silence for a moment, each of them longing for an America they could not reach. Then he watched her as she put on her brassiere.

"I'll call you next week," he said.

"Next week I may not be here," she said. "But try me the week after."

The earthquake hit a few days later, and the next afternoon he rode to Leninakan with the gang at the Institute. Foreigners were not allowed at first, but Gago and Khatchig got him into the bus. "He's one of us," Gago told the official in charge of the bus, "he's Armenian."

The bus curved into the highland with the mountains to the west, the trunk loaded with supplies as if for a camping trip. "You're finally seeing the countryside," Gago said, "*absos*, it has to be like this." His face was beautiful in the

light through the window, his deep eyes and craggy nose like the land itself. He was only twenty-eight then, but his face seemed glazed with history as he pointed to the mountains where he once went on a backpacking trip. Yura, sitting across the aisle, pointed to where he grew up and where his parents still lived. "He's a country bumpkin," Gago joked, and Yura agreed with a big smile. They were all so young and yet were men at the height of their strength and quickness. "I'm hungry," Khatchig said, and he started ripping the bread and sausage.

They called themselves *the brigade*, from *briga*, for strife. They were going to rescue survivors, but the battle would be for the dead. Outside the window the quiet landscape lay like Poseidon himself, his giant body resting peacefully after he had killed and maimed, the little bus crawling the hills like an ant returning to a shattered hive.

It was dusk when they arrived, the broken city dusted pink in the winter haze and the streets clogged with cars and trucks. The bus had to stop on the outskirts and they walked into a frenzy of men who were rushing everywhere like ants who had lost their directions. "Stay behind me!" Gago shouted. He was in charge of the old American who had no legal permission to be here and who stayed behind him in a small group while the rest of the brigade disappeared in the search to be useful.

The small buildings were still standing, but the big ones had cracked or collapsed into mounds of rubble, and dozens of men stood waiting to dig or pass the buckets of dust and stones, the little brigade walking past them as if into a dream.

Khatchig knew the city well and led the way to one of the squares where they could leave their supplies and search for work. The buildings around the square had been government offices and they rushed to one of the mounds that must have been a highrise. It was dark by now and very cold and the only light was from one of the tractors parked on the street, the noise of the motor loud and incessant in the cacophony of yelling and a bright beam focused on the mound like a spotlight for a movie set.

More than a day had passed but the government relief was incompetent, and the swarms of men dug frantically wherever they could squeeze into the beam of light. Joining them, the brigade began to dig with their hands or pass the buckets back and forth, household buckets and toy buckets, so many on the lines they shivered in the cold unable to move. It was better to keep warm by digging despite the futility and the overwhelming dust. They worked or tried to for three hours, but there were too many for the few spots and they finally just stood and watched. No bodies had been uncovered and they stood on the dark mound while the dust seemed to seep into their lungs as if it were the dead themselves.

Around midnight, exhausted and cold, they returned to the camp in the little square across the street. It was full of families huddled around little fires and they made their own fire with scrapwood from the rubble. Gago and Khatchig, not wanting to stop, went to roam the dark streets, but the rest huddled around the fire and turned their faces from the smoke in the changing wind.

About an hour later a truck arrived with bread and bottled water, then Khatchig and Gago returned. They had found a site where everyone could be helpful at the first light of dawn. Waiting until then everyone stared at the flames and rubbed hands and smoked cigarettes like hobos or refugees, a few of them trying to divert the horror with sex jokes which the old one couldn't understand because of his poor vocabulary.

In the cold darkness the other little fires in the square were very beautiful and the families huddled in their camps like glowing figures of a powerful drama. There in the shadows of the little flames the homeless seemed like the ghosts of the genocide in the death march and the stars cowled around them like an eternal audience of suffering.

Sleepless and weary the young brigade passed the hours with bottles of homemade mulberry whiskey and the sex jokes, then they dozed into silence as they squeezed around the flames and held each other up, the old one once again still awake at the hour of the dogwatch most prized by monks for deepest meditation.

Once at the same hour in a Japanese monastery in Bodh Gaya a monk had led the way to a basement where the remaining few would face the wall for the final sitting, and now staring at the embers of the dying flames the one who couldn't sleep remembered that night while the tractor kept droning and the crowds of men kept digging in the mound. So too had he dug for someone in a mound in that monastery when his *I* was so weary and the basement had felt like a burial crypt. After that sitting in the monastery everyone went upstairs for the chanting and the drone of the tractor was like that chanting while the embers of the fire glowed more brilliant in the tiny flames, the chanting growing louder and a monk walking outside to a log by a huge bell and swinging the log into the bell as the chanting reached its climax, the gong resounding over little Bodh Gaya like a giant herald of the sun and the long rays stream- ing into the monastery like the birth of the universe. Such was that dawn in the Bodh Gaya were the Buddha was enlightened.

But there were no rays now and no bell gonged over the rooftops, there was just the tractor droning on and the spar- rows chirping away the darkness into the nacred light of the morning haze, the mound appearing across the street like an exhumated skull.

Then the square came into view with the different fam- ilies exposed to the sky, a statue of Lenin rising above them in the standard pose, its arm raised and the fist pointing to the mound. "The statue of Lenin is still standing," said the American. "Sure," said Gago as he scratched himself awake, "they made sure those statues were built to last, unlike these buildings."

He lit a cigarette and left it in his lips while he rubbed his hands over the embers. He must have smoked a pack since leaving Yerevan. "Eat something," the older man said, as if he were his father. Gago was in fact born the same year he could have had a child himself. "How are you going to work if you smoke instead of eating?" "I'm not hungry," Gago said, "the tea will be enough."

After the tea Khatchig led the way through the quiet streets, and the broken glass crackled under their feet, some jars still stacked in a shop on a corner as if they were walking through Pompeii or an abandoned movie set. "Remember the streets," Gago said, "so you can return to the square in case we get separated, can you read the signs?" "No," said the one who never learned the alphabet, "but I'll remember."

He was as excited now as he was horrified. He had no family or friends in Leninakan and he felt more alien in the world around him than ever before, the broken dreamlike city more real than any in his ordinary life. Sleepless and exhausted, he rushed on as if to catch a performance.

It was in the courtyard with another mound, only this one was smaller. It had been a natal hospital and the digging was now even quicker after a baby was rescued in the night. At the side of the courtyard were about a dozen corpses covered by sheets and the long-faced families sat waiting for more to come.

On the mound the dust was now familiar and the brigade plunged into the digging as if they had been doing it all their lives, then they tied and untied the cables around the concrete slabs and the crane lowered the slabs by the corpses with the wonder of machines and the power over stone. So many stones all pink and grey and the dust in their breath as they hauled away what remained of architecture and engineering, the fragments of floors and ceilings coiled with steel and filled with shredded cloth and splintered furniture, a roll of gauze and a syringe, a little plastic doll.

But where were the bodies, there should have been so many more than the dozen in the courtyard, were they in the dust, were they in his eyes and lungs? *I want to feel a body*, said the part of the artist that was like a Monet who couldn't help studying the play of light on his wife's cadaver, that part that always wanted to feel death and taste it and know it at last, *I want to see someone in all these stones.*

Maybe there was someone alive in the mounds, yet they were really digging for the dead, and in the next few days the sheets and coffins would be everywhere.

They shoveled and hauled for three hours, but still no body had emerged, and by late morning there was less to do after more men had arrived. "Comon," Gago said, "Rupen found some homes nearby where we can be more useful."

Delirious with fatigue and the fascinating horror, he followed Gago and Rupen through the unreal city as if on a acid trip, everywhere bright in the noon sun like a lightning crack between the living and the dead, the crackle of glass beneath the shoes the only sound in the eery quiet. Then suddenly there was Kevorg waving from a corner and the brigade met him halfway.

"Petros," Kevorg said intensely, his face familiar from the Institute and yet not the same Kevorg. He had not been on the bus but had come on his own. He was from Leninakan and he had wanted to bring the visitor here. "I wanted to show you my lovely Leninakan," Kevorg said, "now look at it."

Kevorg was on his way to his home which was only cracked. His family was unharmed and he was helping them to leave. As he talked in the empty street it became both his childhood and the American's in America, each of them looking at the other as if to confirm they were still alive while their childhood memories lay in the rubble and broken glass. "Come," Rupen said, "we have work to do."

A few blocks further they came to a narrow street with four story homes like those in West Hoboken, each home with a different story a child once wanted to know whenever he peeked through the doors to see who lived inside. The homes had collapsed and their lines were curved like a child's drawing. There were a few men working on one of them and some families sat on the sidewalk as they looked up and waited.

The rubble here felt more intimate than at the larger mounds, intimate from *intimare*, to hint, as in a secret, and by now the dust and stones were familiar. One of the men seemed to know where to dig and the one who had grown up in such a home now helped the man tear away the shreds of lathing and plaster. He tried to keep up with the man who worked non-stop, but he almost fainted from fatigue and had to climb down to the street where a woman gave him a bottle of water to clear his throat.

An hour passed as the different relics emerged from the dust like a buried civilization, the shards of dishes and splinters of furniture and dusty clothes and toys and more toys, so many toys and fragments that could be imagined into anything now laid aside for the garbage or the recycling pile, but no body nor face of a miracle.

Then the man who knew where to dig wanted to focus on a certain spot and he hurried more than before. They dug through the dust and hauled away the scraps of plaster and lathing and linoleum, then the one who had been searching for someone all his life was on his knees stretching into a jagged hole like into a secret and the hem of dress suddenly appeared and an instant later a knee and a bicep. "Oh!" the man cried looking over his shoulder, "Oh!" he kept crying as he turned away with his face in his hands.

She must have been about eleven or twelve, her leg emerging from the dust with an intimacy only the dead can offer. *Touch her,* said that same voice as at the natal hospital, *touch her leg and uncover her face.*

"Come away!" Gago yelled, and he pulled at the digger not wanting him to look because he didn't want to look. *Let me dig,* the digger wanted to say, *I need to see her face.* "Come!" Gago kept saying, and he kept pulling as if to pull himself away. "Our work is done," Gago said. *No,* said a silent voice, *I need to see her face, I need to see her face,* and the voice kept scraping away the plaster and the wood, but the girl's torso was buried under a beam and it would take hours to pull her out. Then feeling embarrassed as if she were more alive than before he touched her leg and when he felt its coldness he wanted to keep touching and feeling as if his fingers could revive her.

"Let's stay and help to pull her out," he said. "No," Gago said, horrified, "there will be others for that." Gago had friends in Leninakan and she could have been one of them. She had been the niece of the man who was now crying on the other side of the rubble. She had a face and a name and was like all the children the one who never had a child had always loved.

Too embarrassed of his motive to disobey Gago, he let himself be pulled away and they climbed down to the street. *But I needed to see her face,* the voice kept saying, *I needed to see her face.*

Back in the camp there was some food from a supply truck. A few of the brigade had returned earlier and Yura was roasting potatoes in the fire, his face so bright and the potatoes so delicious under the charred skin, the bottled water so soothing to a parched throat and everyone so alive in the middle of the dead.

The foreign help was finally arriving after the Soviet delays and the excavation would be better organized. More men were also arriving from the rest of the country and they increased the surplus of diggers. None of the small brigade wanted to leave, but they had no groundcloths or sleeping bags, and unable to go sleepless another night they returned to Yerevan to rest.

Back in the dorm Stella was in the lobby and wanted news. She was a vibrant young Iranian-Armenian anthropologist who was eager to join the relief, not only out of compassion but to be part of the action. "I want to go," she said. "Why?" said the one who had just returned. "What do you mean, why?" she said. "There's not much we can do," he said, "they need experienced people." "But at least you were there," she said. Then, as if she were clairvoyant, she said, "You touched the stones." "Yes," he said, "I touched the stones."

Up on the third floor Gunter was in Paul's room and they were eating liver and onions with fresh bread and vodka. "We have some extra," Paul said. "No, thanks," he said, "I want to wash, is there any hot water?" "Yes," Gunter said, "you're lucky, it came today."

They had wanted to go on one of the brigades, but foreigners were not allowed and Gunter was relieved. "I've never seen a dead person in my life," Gunter said, "I'm thirty-four years old and I've never even been in a funeral parlor."

His own room was the same yet no longer solid, and when he washed in the tub the dust flowed into the drain and the drain led to the pipes and the pipes went into the walls and down the floors through the same kind of lathing and plaster as in Leninakan, the soap and the mirror floating in a phenomena that would one day crumble into another mound.

Then as he lay in bed in the darkness the girl returned like a girl in a dream, her leg emerging from the dust and her arm beneath a broken stud.

In the morning the doves were waiting for the wheatberries where he fed them on the windowsill. How beautiful were their violets and grays in the winter light and the little white beneath their tails, their eyes like ebony. In the distance the apartment buildings lay in cubes of pink and blue like a peaceful Cezanne with a buried torso in montage.

By evening the brigade was back in the camp in fresh underwear as if they had come home again. By now the wooden coffins were everywhere and they were like reminders that this was still a city and not yet a Pompeii or museum.

Searching again for where they could be useful they walked through the darkness and the different districts felt peaceful and intimate like a childhood fantasy of wandering anywhere one wanted without cops or laws.

Then they came to a huge mound as wide as a football field. A complex of highrises all fell together and dozens of men were digging wherever the lights could reach and the sea of dust was like a giant dump.

At one spot he dug into what must have been a large closet and he pulled away a string of coats that must have belonged to a wealthy woman who had a taste for fur and Persian lamb, each of them emerging from the dust as if from a magician's fist, coat after coat but no flesh or bone and the different pelts lying in a pile as if alive.

Then Gago reached into the dust and found a little book with a Russian title. "It's by Hegel," he said, thumbing through the pages. "It's a collection of works by Hegel."

"Have you ever read Hegel?"

"No, we were supposed to in school because of Marx, but I never did, have you ever read Hegel?"

"No, I never did either."

"Well," Gago said, "whoever did won't need him anymore." And he flipped the book back into the rubble, his beautiful young beard now dusted grey in the bluish light like a Dante standing on the mound of the dead.

"What are you doing?" Gago said, "why are you putting that stone in your pocket?"

"It's a *hishadag* (souvenir), I always take a stone, ever since I was a kid."

"You want a souvenir of death?"

"I don't know of what, of something I don't know."

"Let's get back to work, we're not here for souvenirs."

They slept a few hours in a bus that night. The driver kept the heater on and they curled next to each other in the double seats as if they were travelling somewhere. They slept only about two hours but it was enough, and when they woke it was dawn and they looked for work again.

It was Sunday, four days after the quake. Survivors seemed unlikely by now, but news of success increased their strength and they walked to another part of the city. "Look!" Yura said, pointing to a big yellow crane, "the Japanese have come."

Then they came to where two Swiss volunteers talked German to a local interpreter, and everyone stood back so the dogs could sniff in the mounds. The dogs were big beautiful shepherds and as they panted and sniffed for the odor of life everyone admired their animal grace, but their barking was not the proper kind. "They're very tired," the Swiss volunteer told the interpreter in German, "they've been held up in Moscow all night and they had no sleep."

They wandered to another district where the mound had been a primary school, and there were about a dozen coffins on the street and a supply of gas masks, but the masks weren't needed because the bodies were frozen and the odor still faint. It was a sweet sick odor like skunk, and it lingered over the coffins in the frosty air.

They tried to work, but then they just sat on the side drinking tea and smoking cigarettes with the other workers, the coffins only a few yards away. One of the other workers was a jolly old peasant who wanted to hear stories about America, and his smiles seemed to say there was no shame in feeling well in the middle of gloom. He had come to work and now he was resting and drinking tea. "Do they have quakes this big in America?" he asked.

There were blankets and canvas when they returned to camp, and Gago said he would stay another night. "But you go back with Araik," he said, "you're too sick to stay." Gago was right, he had caught a cold in the fatigue and stress, so he followed Araik to the busses in the main square.

They weaved through the chaos and Araik almost found a ride, but a crowd was yelling and shaking fists in the face of the driver who had tripled the rate while others drove for free, the driver standing by his door as if to say he was looking out for number one.

Then Araik found another bus that would be passing through Yerevan on its way south. It was already full of workers from a commune but the workers let the two squeeze in.

The workers knew that Araik was different by his gentle speech, yet everyone seemed equal like soldiers in battle. Araik was a good but poor artist who barely raised a family with his art, and they were from a vineyard and winery. Araik gave them the canned fish from the brigade and the workers shared their sausage and the camaraderie was warm and soothing as the bus climbed into the snowy landscape, the Turkish border just a few miles away and the quake now part of history like the genocide.

Back at the dorm old Khosrov, the evening clerk, was sitting at his desk in his grey overcoat and the what were they called Russian hat with the fur flaps, his rac-

coon eyes peering over the counter and his deep voice rasping from the underworld of his cigarette lungs. He was an old vet who had survived the Stalin years and he supplemented his pension by sitting here like a furry witness to the in and out of life. "You have a message from Stella," he said.

Stella had finally found a ride as an interpreter and she had taken a call for the Fulbright lecturer before she left. *"Harry Smith,"* she wrote, *"wants to talk with you. He's from CBS and he will call again tomorrow. The phones are so bad he will have to keep trying."*

The cold turned into a fever, but it was gone after a long sleep, and in the morning he felt drugged by his body's cure against the virus. Snow had fallen during the night and outside the window the bare city was vivid in the fresh white.

Downstairs in the lobby he tried calling an official to become an interpreter and when the official finally came through the phone he said the roads were closed and no one else would be allowed. Five days had passed since the quake and there was a supposed to be threat of disease from the corpses. "What disease?" Shooshig said in English. She was a Syrian-Armenian studying math at the university. "There's not going to be any disease, the bodies are all frozen, they just don't want us to go, it's the usual Soviet crap."

It was cold in the lobby but warm by the heater, and he wrote his journal sitting next to old Hripsimeh, the day clerk in charge of the good phone that she would keep clear in case Harry Smith got through, some dorm students playing ping-pong and some others yelling into the bad phone trying to be heard, old Guyana cooking *tannabur* in the buffet and Ararat the commandant watching the news with his cronies in his office. Everyone knew someone who died and everywhere was alive from the great slap in the face.

When the mail arrived he got a telegram from Hass back in Berkeley. *"Peter,"* it said, *"are you all right?"* It must have cost Hass about twenty bucks and he felt indebted to him for his kindness. Then Mufid, the Syrian graduate student, came in from the cold and shook his pink and chubby cheeks. "Is terrible," he said in English, "you see it?" "Yes, I saw it." "Is terrible, no?" "Yes, it was terrible." "Terrible," he said, the *b* delicious on his Arabic tongue, his beautiful Arab eyes expressive and bright.

"Come," Hripsimeh said in Armenian, "come eat *tannabur* with me." She lay the bowls on the desk with the *tutvatz* and then unfolded the big sheets of the fresh flatbread that was not sold in the shops but baked by someone she knew around the corner, the same kind as in the villages in Turkey.

He told her about Turkey and she said her mother was from Kharpert. She was bundled up in several layers of sweaters and socks and her old face was beautiful, a few teeth missing in her smile and a scarf around her neck. Like old Khatchig she was retired from working in a factory, but she originally came from a village and grew up with flatbread. She tore it apart and stuffed it with cheese and chewed it with her side teeth as she slurped the *tannabur.* The *tannabur* was cooked with the same wheatberries he fed the doves on the windowsill and it was sprinkled with mint like in his childhood. It was a good hot soup and the *tutvatz* of pickled cabbage and hot peppers made it even more delicious. Then the phone finally rang and the voice of a Harry Smith came through the static and the odors of the yoghurt and vinegar.

Harry Smith was a newsmonger who gathered suffering and sold it like produce for dinnertimes. People on the other side of the world wanted it as the journal keeper always did, and like him they would buy televisions to watch it instead of eating in silence. Should his shame say no? *No, you can't have this suffering,* a part of him wanted to say, *I don't want it to pay your million dollar salaries.*

Instead another part of him talked with Harry Smith as if the world needed his voice even at the price of making him a fool. "Listen," Harry Smith said with the smoothness of his trade, "this is going to be transmitted live and I want you to tell us your personal feelings." "My personal feeling in three minutes?" "Well, do the best you can," Harry Smith said.

And so he talked while Hripsimeh looked up listening to his English babble as if he knew what he was talking about. "What did you tell him?" she asked afterwards. "I don't know," he said.

Two days later Stella returned to the dorm. She had interpreted for a group of English firemen and they had rescued a little girl who had been buried alive in one of the mounds. She had talked to the girl, she said, she had looked down into the hole and comforted the girl while the firemen dug her out. She was very tired now but her face was bright with the rescue. She had touched the stones and now her name would be in *Newsweek*. She paused and looked out the window as she remembered one of the mounds. A family had wanted to know about the bodies of their relatives and she had translated the question to one of the firemen. "He told me," she said gravely, "that when a building that big comes down, all that's left of a body is hair. Now how was I supposed to translate that?"

On the street Vartuhi from the university said she lost a whole family of cousins, and Henrik shook his head over his. The woman in the bakery across the street lost her sister and young Zovig wept for her grandmother as a trolley rattled through the intersection, the passing faces full of life and the sparrows angelic on the bare branches.

By midweek the cold was in its peaceful phase of slow motion and a husky voice. Where was Sirpuhi? She was late again.

When she finally came her foot was bruised because she had fallen while running back home to get her identification card which she had to show old Khatchig before he could allow her upstairs. The lobby was full of young Russian volunteers who had been sleeping on the floor and she limped through them to meet her client by the steps. "I'm sorry I'm late," she said. "That's okay," he said, "I'm glad to see you."

On the second floor one of the common rooms was packed with leftovers from the American relief teams, and there were stacks of toilet paper among the cans of macaroni and beans which were left for the refugees. To ask for some paper would have been too embarrassing. Gunter would hitch a flight to West Germany with the German relief team and then return with some extra rolls along with toothpaste and condoms. They were reminders of comfort in the west, yet how expensive Sirpuhi would be there.

She had drunk some *champagnski* somewhere and she was turned on, but her old client couldn't make her come. She squirmed and stretched and crawled all over him until she finally said, "I can't, you don't have to try anymore, come, you make yourself happy."

With death everywhere his hunger seemed to feel more intense, as if this were the last time it could be gratified. Afterwards, in the pulse of the quiet, she asked about the little stone souvenir by the lamp. When she put it back it made a little shadow under the light like a piece of art in a museum. Did she know anyone in Leninakan, he asked? Of course, she said, everyone knew someone from Leninakan, but she didn't want to talk about them. Her flesh was warm and alive and the little vein in her neck was like a lifeline of her sweetness, the silence of the room pulsing with the memory of the mounds and nothing left but hair, her long black hair luxuriant in the lamplight like a gift from the deep.

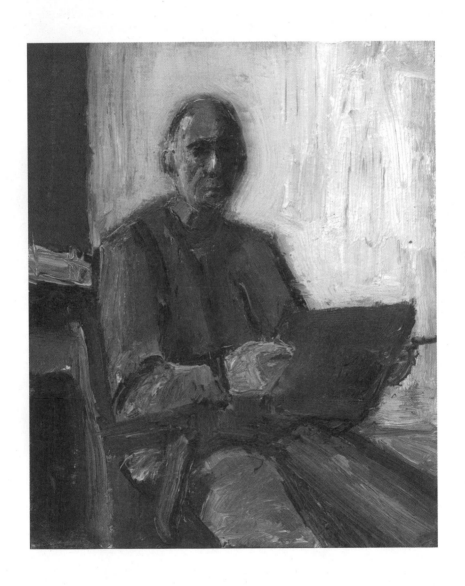

THE GREAT AMERICAN LONELINESS

THE GIRL III

The winter passed and spring filled with tours of the countryside and ghosts of monks in the rocky monasteries, the canyons like Colorado and the lake of Sevan like Tahoe and Louise. "Come," said Migurdich when he took his American cousin there one weekend, "let's climb the hill."

It rose in a lovely dingle full of flowers, and from its top they could see the lake as it fanned to the horizon with the hills to the side, the new grass a juicy green from the winter wetness. Then looking down into the dell they watched the girls gather herbs in a scene so luminous they seemed eternal, their little figures like the flowers as they filled their sacks with the different tastes for salads and soups, lemony or sweet or deliciously bitter.

But the high of the climb led to staring and sinking into thought. "I'm going to miss you so much," Migurdich said, "why don't you stay here, you don't seem at home in America?"

"I can't stay here, Migurdich, I'm not at home wherever I go."

"Why is that?"

"I don't know why."

"I know why you're not at home."

"Why am I not at home?"

"Because you live alone and have no wife and children."

"I have no wife and children because I'm not at home, if I were at home I would have them.

"I too feel not at home sometimes."

"Why is that, my cousin?"

"Sometimes I wonder what it's all about, you work hard, you raise children, and then what?"

"Then you watch your children raise children."

"Is that all there is?"

"I don't know, I don't even have that much."

"You stay here. We can come to this hill and talk about such things."

"Good old Migurdich. Tell me about your childhood. Were you at home growing up?"

"Oh yes. We were very poor but we were always together. Did I ever tell you about the time I almost drowned?"

"No, tell me."

Back in Yerevan it was the middle of April, and from his dormitory room the one who was not at home could see in the yard the little lamb who bleated and pulled the cord that was tied around its neck. Then a father came out of the shanty and sliced its neck and when the bowl was filled with blood he dipped his fingers into the redness and painted a cross on his son's forehead.

It was April of the anniversary of the genocide and another tribe gathered to remember it like the Jews remembered theirs, their own genocide tying them so tight it seemed sometimes that had not so many been slaughtered there would be no Israel and that Hitler was the father of their new nation,

It was April of the young grape leaves filled with rice and the lamb sizzling in an aromatic barbecue.

It was April of the long walk to the river and the fire on the hill, but he, whose father's brothers had their necks sliced like a lamb's, waited until the sundown after the crowd was gone.

It was a walk like those in Belle Isle by the Detroit River and by the Thames and the Tiber and the Tigris and the Ganges, his voice speaking to a void as if it were a girl in a vision whose face was always hidden. Now at least he had touched her leg.

Then he came to the bridge the German prisoners of war helped build by carrying the stones for the arch. They had struggled until the end of the war and at night they carved crosses and toys for the little Armenian kids who gave them food in return. That was history, but it was not recorded in the books.

The bridge led into the trees and he climbed the hill as if it were a history of prisoners and a cross a father wiped on his son's forehead, his destination the fire of decapitated uncles and those who died in the desert.

He climbed into the trees as if they were the nightmares of a Nazi and a Turk each hungry for blood. He was that

Nazi and Turk who climbed into the knots of his own hatred, his eyes tight with vengeance and his throat locked by a scream he could not let go.

It was time to let go, it was time to break the spell, his life was at stake, a Turk was killing his uncle and a Nazi was climbing the fire-escape. Deeper and deeper he climbed into the muscles of his rage and his lungs filled with hurt, rage rooted in hurt and hurt rooted in rage as each breath untied the knots like an old monk in a basement and a shovel in a mound, the drone of memory like a tractor by the dead. *Make it go away!* cried a child in a darkness, *oh please make it go away!*

But his voice became its own fury and the silence shouted back at him. *You, you, you, and you,* he cried, but the trees were his only audience. *You hurt me, you abused me, you insulted me. . . . Oh leave me alone,* he cried to his hatred, *please leave me alone!*

Yet he kept climbing and his breath kept digging like a relentless monk and a shovel in the stones, step by step in the burning of hatred while the scream lay locked inside. *Stay with the pain,* said an old monk. *I can't,* cried a child, *I can't.*

But he could and with each step his breath kept digging until each knot was untied and the scream exploded like the mushroom of a holocaust, the photographs scattered by the broken walls and the beloved crushed to dust.

There was no one left now, nothing but the breeze through the trees and the quiet calm of another sundown, the horizon bleeding into a soft blue. No more you or fury but just the breeze and his muscles stretching to embrace the nearest tree. It was more than a tree, it was . . . *Let me hold you, let me touch you, let me see your face.*

Then came the wound itself that was now a grief so deep it lay buried in the very center of his being like an ego on a cross, grief and more grief as if it were its own vulture eating its own entrails, grief for his own rage that now caved his lungs like a broken temple and twisted his muscles into a crippled father who waited for a child to come home after school.

He was now his own father he once kicked in the shin with a child's rage against his impotence, he was the wound that now churned his navel and opened him into the crying.

He cried, he cried the crying of the ages as if his wound and his cure were the same, his navel churning in the great purge while he hugged the tree as if the void would crush him to nothingness should he let go.

But he didn't let go and he kept hugging the tree until the crying left him limp upon a shore by the shipwreck of his life.

When he opened his eyes he expected a wasteland, but there appeared instead a strange and familiar wood where everywhere was fresh and clear as if he were a child again, the peaceful calm like the love he had longed for all his life and the tree rising like a witness. He touched the bark as if it were his soul and it rose into the branches like his breath deepening into forgiveness. No more pain and no more rage but just the flow of his breath as if he were the flow and the flow were him.

Then in the wanting to keep the flow it disappeared, and he continued climbing the hill until he remembered he hadn't said goodbye to the tree, but when he looked back there were all alike and he couldn't find the one he had hugged.

When he reached the monument there were only a few latecomers like himself, and he walked with them around the fire of those who died in The Great Hatred. It was a big fire and it was kept burning all year long and every April everyone came and lay a flower in remembrance, but he had no flower and he just stared at the flames as if they were the uncles and aunts he had never known.

He was tired, he was so very tired of it all, all the flowers of his longing and the photos of who married who and who their children married, yet their ghosts followed him down the hill to the dormitory and the return to America, a young moon in the sundown like a little girl who had become a Persephone.

He had once embraced her in a dream, but a wound swallowed her into the dead and she reigned there like despair until she rose again after the burning. How beautiful she was, but he would have to die before he could see her face.

THE AKI

Travelling through Turkey years ago, I came to Adana on the circle back to Istanbul, but my foot was swollen from a bad burn and I stayed only two nights, nothing left of my mother's childhood except the bridge. The *aki* had been on the other side of the river and she had often told me of sitting on the donkey when her family went there in the spring. "Look for the bridge," she had said before I left, "and you will find it." But when I hobbled there it led to more highrises and traffic, so I just sat on a bench to rest my foot and I watched a boy fishing in the sundown. "You stayed in Adana only two days?" she would say. "My foot was bad, Ma, and I had to get back to Istanbul." "Well, at least you saw my Adana."

Not really, except for the bridge and the boy fishing from its ancient stones, the river flowing fresh from the mountains through the gentle arches to the sea, the boy and the stones and the river all glowing in the long rays. "I remember the bridge," she always said. "I sat on the donkey and we crossed it to our *aki* on the other shore.

Tas Kopru, said the guide book, and she too had used the Turkish word, *kopru.* It was built by Hadrian and later restored by Justinian. The Crusader, Geoffrey of Bouillon, crossed it on his way to Palestine. It was the bridge of history and the *aki* lay buried in its nightmare, but the river was the same and the same light shined on the boy with his line in the waves. Here now in this screen, I fish with my own lines as if they could be a movie of the lost *aki* with my longing like a zoom.

Here in my movie, are my mother's family and their donkey crossing the bridge, their figures silhouetted in the morning sun like a Daumier. She can't remember their faces, but she remembers her mother had red and freckled cheeks, and her father was a gentle man whose heels were cracked like hers are now. They were peasants like those of Daumier and Millet and Van Gogh, and their clothes were in earth tones and patches of primal color, the little Zaroohe and her younger brother in a donkey cart and the donkey's hooves clicking on the cobbles, the wheels creaking in counterpoint.

But there was no cart. She doesn't remember any cart, she was alone on the donkey. Then how did her little brother come? Maybe there were two trips, maybe she came on the second trip? Yet there has to be a cart so they can be filmed together. They are returning to their place in the sun after huddling in a tenement all winter, the rains have ended and the fields are splashed with wildflowers in the new green.

What kind of wildflowers? Are they the lupen and broom of California and Provence, and are there poppies too? A Faulkner or Tolstoy could find the details of their stories in the world around them, but mine are buried under highrises and gas stations.

Yet the climate is the same as California and Provence and the rains are only in winter, the fields full of fruit and cotton and sesame and flax. It is like a happy day in childhood before my loneliness began, the father a whole man like a thriving specie before the clear cut and genocide, the mother like a glowing dream before the day brought back the night. Shut your eyes to see, they say, and come home again.

They road goes east to Urfa and Hadjin where the parents were born. They probably met through relatives and settled by Adana after they married. Who knows how they got the *aki*, but it is theirs now and all it needs is hard work.

Home again, says the young mother in Turkish, the bubbly syllables I never learned now translated in subtitles. *Parkes-der—Praise the lord*, says the father in Armenian, though like his wife he spoke only Turkish.

He was a church-going man, but there would be no church until they returned to the city. The metal and the fabric are from the city, but not the wood for the fire nor the food from the vines. Nor is there a dome or a spire or a priest or a mullah, the sons not yet men who will kill each other and the daughter not yet a prize, there is just love and light and the need to live in them, for this is the home in the dream that says we don't have to wander anymore.

"Look, Papa," says the oldest boy, *"the fig tree has grown."* It is as if he is looking at himself in the new green of his life. His Armenian name is Boghos, like the Greek for Paul, and indeed this is the home of the famous Paul of the very religion that would lead to death, the very naming and the tongue itself a part of death. Death is everywhere, and this

is their last year in the *aki*, the fig tree to fall like the orchards in Fresno now paved with developments. Yet here in this vision it curls its limbs with new leaves as if in welcome, and the billowing clouds are an ecstatic white in a brilliant blue.

First comes an open space lined with mulberry trees, then the cabin at the end of it. No, not a cabin, she said. They didn't sleep in it, they just kept their things there, they slept in the open on the deck.

"But what about the road, was it like our roads or was it a dirt road?" "You ask too many questions, be glad I can remember this much."

So it is just a road as in a Ruysdael or a Bellini, its vanishing point an eternal *au revoir*. And here now in the *aki* itself, the peach and apricot are in bloom and soon the quince and mulberry, or is the mulberry already blooming? What do mulberry trees look like, mulberry as in Hemingway's story where the silk worms feed in the middle of the night when he couldn't sleep? And did they wake with petals falling on their faces?

They are falling now, pink and white and stippled with yellow and a delicate red, the young Zaroohe and her younger brother let loose to play and maybe her older brother as well, for loving parents would let their children play as long as they wanted, the time for work will come later, if they live long enough.

They unpack, and the young mother—she couldn't have been more than thirty if her oldest boy is twelve—airs the bedrolls on the line. Did they bring the bedrolls from the city, or did they have two sets, one for the city and one for the *aki*?

And the shack, who built it and with what kind of wool? They don't sleep in it because there is no rain, and the nights are as pleasant as in Avignon or New Delhi. Mosquitoes? Maybe a few but not a hindrance in the cool nights, so they sleep in the open with the deck raised high and the donkey underneath. What a pleasure it must have been to sleep under the stars with no streetlamps of insomnia, the love of stars zooming like a *Voyager* into a sparkling infinity! Listen, it says, listen to the crickets like their echo on earth, their incessant rhythm like a Tibetan prayer wheel. How peacefully my humble family sleeps on their bedrolls.

What kind of bedrolls? Where they of the wool the immigrants brought to America like the quilt here now on my bed? How magical it was one summer when my mother washed the wool and I helped her card it on the roof, the forked branch like a tuning fork as if I were making music. How bountiful it was, like a gift from sheep to protect us from the cold darkness. Feel it, says the sense of touch no movie can simulate, touch the woolen quilt to be part of life and never be alone again.

But maybe the blankets weren't wool.

"I don't remember seeing sheep, we lived in a land of cotton."

Then let them be of cotton, the same as on the way to Fresno in the autumn with tiny puffs bursting from their starry husks, the cotton of this shirt and a weary seamstress in a sweatshop.

"One night I saw my mother and father making love. I never told you this before because I was ashamed, but now it doesn't matter. We all slept together and when I woke one night I saw them, but I didn't know what it meant."

They sigh in counterpoint to the humming crickets, two small people with their genitals together like hairy animals.

"My mother was pregnant when we started the march, and the baby died on the road."

Not yet, not yet, let the petals fall on their sleep once more, let me guard over them like a god with the moon in his hair, my zoom rising higher until not only they but all such families come in view, their dreams purling into the clouds that blanket our tiny planet. They dream, they dream the dream of life as if it is a movie for an audience of stars, all dreams a cinema in a giant dome of wish-fulfillments, the crickets leading to birds like strings to woodwinds in a symphony and the darkness dissolving into a luscious blue, the morning star cradled by an old moon and the silhouette of trees embroidered in the glowing crimson. Wake up, it is not time to die.

The father is the first to rise, or maybe the mother or one of the children who stands on the platform as if on the deck of a ship, the dawn like the other shore. And now the long rays of the new sun are shredded by the leaves. Come, says the need to piss, let the piss flow in the vineyard and then wash from the pump with the water of life, it is time to break bread around the teapot.

"We sweetened the tea with syrup, our breakfast was sweetened tea and bread."

It is the syrup from last year's harvest, the big ceramic jars sealed with fig leaves and mud. But were they left here over the winter? Did no one come and take them?

There was another family who lived in a tent by the road and they must have guarded the *aki* during the winter. They were black and landless, yet life is home to those who share it and make more. "I remember their children."

"Paint my *aki*," she said when she saw me struggling with a canvas in her garage one day. "I'll describe it and you paint it."

"I can't paint like that, Ma, I need something to look at."

"What kind of an artist are you if you can't paint from imagination? Be like that painting teacher in the television, she just paints and leaves it, but you keep wiping it away."

"I'm not as good as she is."

"Oh you always say you're not good as someone, you don't have to be as good as anyone, you just have to do it."

"You do it."

"All right, give me that brush, and I'll do it myself."

And so for the first time in her life, she held the brush like a ladle and dabbed with her fearless and matter of fact way a few marks on the primed paper as if she were a kindergarten girl.

"What's that, Ma?"

"What do you mean, what's that? That's a tree, don't you know what a tree looks like?"

"Okay, it's a tree. Now let's put some more paint on the brush."

"No, I don't like that color, it's too grey. Give me some yellow for the shack."

And so with the yellow she made a little shelter like children everywhere, then she added the road with the primal flatness that is always fresh and alive.

"There," she said, handing back the brush, "you see how easy it is?"

"That's pretty good, Ma. Why don't I leave some paint and paper and you can do more after I leave?"

"What's the matter with you, I don't have time for painting, you see all the cleaning I have to do."

"You said your brother used to draw. It will make you remember your brother."

"I already remember my brother."

He sits under the mulberry tree like a young Sidhartha practicing for enlightenment, his daily lesson the lights and darks and his delicate lines like the fine hairs above his lips, Uncle Boghos, the *gh* pronounced from the back of the palate as if clearing the throat, the *Bo* and the *os* like a call from the deep, the boy who never became a man and nothing known of him but that he loved to draw.

"Make lines, my boy, make lines," said Ingres to the young Degas, *"keep making lines."* What for, said an old artist who had saved them all, what for when no one will see them? *"For Eden,"* said Blake, for Uncle Boghos who is the love of drawing and seeing a pattern in the lights and darks.

But why is he not helping his father tie the vines or weed the seedling vegetables, how will he survive if he doesn't learn how to farm, what future is there under a mulberry tree with a pad and pencil? Yet his father must have encouraged him, for he too must have been a dreamer.

"I remember my father saying, '*Gyun dolmazdan, nahlar doghar.*'"

"What does it mean?" "It means 'Tomorrow is happening while we sleep and dream.'"

In the vineyard now, he ties the vines and. . . . And what? What was a real father like, a whole man whose hands could tie a world together, who could actually speak instead of groan? Can a movie be made with a shattered memory like the scraps Picasso made into people and animals, a tool for a face and a jar for a torso?

"I remember my brother Boghos telling me to tell him the truth after I broke his pencil. 'If you tell the truth I won't hit you,' he said, 'but if you lie, I will.'" And I told him the truth. 'Yes,' I said, 'I broke your pencil.' " "Is that all you remember?" "Be glad I can remember that much."

She naps in her living room eighty years later, my own pencil following her wrinkles like the map of her life. Who would her brother have been had he survived, he and the others who disappeared under the great eraser?

He sits under the mulberry tree with his little sister playing nearby. She doesn't remember him playing with her because he probably didn't, she was in her own barefoot world with leaves and bugs.

And over there in an open space her mother is sealing another jar with fig leaves and mud, her father picking the last of the toma- toes in the garden.

OLD 2. NAPPING
SLEEP NOON
TANVARS '94

For already in just a few pages the summer is gone and the harvest a syrup to sweeten the winter tea. It has been another summer of details now hiding behind her eyelids like rare species from extinction, the vegetables cooked on an open fire and the yoghurt from the milk of the neighbor's cow, the cracked wheat boiled into bulghur and the dried syrup stripped from sheets like edible leather, a mere minute of flashbacks that must somehow flower from an old woman's nap and come to life in a storyboard.

The father turns the compost and the mother empties the mash, the sun low and the light soft like in Millet's *Gleaners*, the yellowing leaves like a warm dream of life's lushness. There behind her wrinkled eyelids a summer has ripened into glowing ochres and the shadows pulse in violets and reds. It has been a summer like a long life and there are still more grapes on the hairy vines, their juice so sweet it could erase a millennium of bitterness. It has been the summer of life for all who have known its bitter winters and its labor in the vineyard.

A summer as in my own childhood when she treated my father and me to the fresh air of a chicken farm and the odor of chickenshit. She was only forty-four then, and she had saved enough from the factory for two months in Dickran's little chickenfarm in Freehold, which was about an hour from West Hoboken in the truck Vahan drove on his drycleaner's route. Dickran was Vahan's older brother and Vahan was the husband of Manooshag who was my father's niece. Manooshag and Vahan tried to live on that chicken farm during the Depression and when they couldn't anymore they let Dickran have it. Dickran lived alone in that big house and was glad to have us. He was only around sixty then but he seemed ancient, and with my love of father figures I went with him to town to sell his eggs in his ancient pickup with the crankstart, his husky hands on the wheel of the old jalopy as it chugged along the road at the pace of a

Buddha's breathing. It was the last summer of my golden age and I can still smell the chickenshit and the tomatoes heavy on the vines, I can still see the haughty chickens walking on the porch and my mother chasing them with the broom, my paralyzed father sitting silent with his hand in his lap. It was the last year in which I can remember a happiness and I was the same age as my mother when she was torn from her own little Eden.

There were fruit trees on that farm and the sap would drip and harden into a lovely amber on their limbs. She peels the same sap from her own trees now and chews it like a jujube. "What are you doing, Ma?" "Oh, I used to do this on the *aki*."

It has an the amber glow like a late Degas where the features blur but the forms are solid, it is in this glow that my little family sits on the ground for their last meal in the *aki* before their return to the city and the start of the genocide.

They all eat from the same pot and the donkey munches in the background, their dialogue like the voices of silence in a museum without walls.

The mother, Tirfandah, like all the figures from Hatshepsut to Matisse, her freckles a glaze to the eternal feminine.

The father, Haritun, like El Greco's old man in the Met, though he is only in his thirties in the death march.

The brother, Boghos, staring back like a young Picasso with eyes in a mirror as if in a skull.

The child, Toros, unremembered except for his death in Damascus, his grave like a last supper in a peeling fresco.

The little Zaroohe, the sole survivor, her passport photo the only view of what she may have looked like, yet how girls change after nightmare in puberty.

They sit now, still glowing in the sundown, the trees embroidered in the gold leaf of the long rays.

"What are you going to do today," she asked over the phone this morning.

"My work," I said.

"Me too," she said. "I have so much cleaning to do."

22 MAR 99

HARVEST

How beautiful were the apples when I climbed the tree, each a jewel in the yellowing leaves and the branches like arms. How good to be part of life and to taste the light shredded by the leaves, to be at home with open arms like the *Glad Day* of Blake, each apple leading to another. Then came the climb down.

"Richard Yates is dead," Alan had said, "he died several years ago, didn't you know that?"

Alan's beard was grey and he read his book reviews on NPR, but he was still the same Alan who shared his room at 38 Prosper Street by the Rutgers campus.

"Did I ever tell you what this crazy Armenian did to me?" he said to Leo as we sat together. "I was with William Sloane who was the adviser of our undergrad magazine, and I was wearing my jacket that this trusted roommate of mine had borrowed the night before. Bill had said something I needed to write on a pad and when I reached into my pocket for a pen I pulled out a hypodermic needle! 'Ahem,' Bill coughed, 'are you a diabetic, Alan?' 'No,' I said, 'my roommate must have left it here.' "

"I didn't know you're a diabetic," Leo said to me.

"Some diabetic," Alan said. "It was for his heroin."

"Not my heroin, it was Betty Hippy's heroin."

"Betty Hippy?" Leo said with his Santa Claus smile.

"That was her nickname, but not like the word years later, this was in '60 when hip meant hipster. She was an adventurous young woman and she had broken curfew at Douglas College to take me to a jazz club in Manhattan. That was around the time I introduced you to Richard, Alan."

"No," said Alan who usually knew everyone first, "how could that be?"

"I met Richard the year before when I lived in the Village and took a workshop at the New School. Richard was the teacher. He was about your age, Leo, he must have been only in his thirties then. He was working on his first novel, *Revolutionary Road*. I was too young to appreciate it then, but it's really good, isn't it, Alan? Are his later ones just as good?

"*Easter Parade* is better," Alan said.

"I think so too," said Leo, whose own story had just won the O. Henry prize.

"How do you two know each other?" Alan asked Leo and me.

"Leo was very good to me when I moved out here."

"Then you must know Gold through Leo," Alan said.

"No, I used to give Herb a ride to Stanford when he ran the seminar for the Stegner fellows. Later I learned that Herb and Leo had been friends since they were kids. It's like a tree, isn't it, how we all know each other who know others who know everyone else?"

But that night, returning here through the darkness, the ghost of Richard became the moon above the sea, and it fused with the other Richard who had killed himself, the two so different in person and yet similar in pain, each exiting through a bruised apple like in Lawrence's *Ship Of Death*.

A few days later, as if an angel had been to Telegraph Avenue, I found a used copy of *Easter Parade* in Moe's

Books, and tucking it under my arm I walked back here through the empty streets as if it were Richard himself. Six dollars for Richard's sake, said my pennypinching, six dollars for thirty-three years ago when Richard lived in that basement studio on the corner near Seventh and Bleeker in the West Village, the basement bare but for the desk and the bed and a small bookcase, nothing in the tiny kitchen but instant coffee and a bottle of bourbon. Are those the only books he has, I thought? Everyone else's pad had stacks of them like trophies and I myself was stealing them like apples from the new Paperback Gallery, for those were the years when the new kinds were just coming out with good print and paper.

And what else, what else could I remember of that powerful spring when the famous Norman Mailer lived around the corner on Perry Street and was on the march to save Caryl Chessman or in the Blue Note listening to Mingus? Richard was not famous like Mailer and had published just a few stories, yet I would visit him for wisdom as if he were. *"Madame Bovary,"* he said, *"Madame Bovary." Madame*

Bovary what, what did he say about *Madame Bovary?* Try to remember, says my need now to write a memoir about the tree of artisthood, try to remember what he said in the basement or in *Chumley's Pub* the night he brought me along for a drink. Is all that's left of him a jar of *Nescafe* and a night in *Chumley's?*

I just found the letter he sent me after I had returned to college, the words meaning so much more now. He was only in his mid-thirties then and I was only twenty, but he was the older writer and I looked up to him. *"Take it easy,"* he said, for I had just returned from Mexico where I had hitched like a Hemingway to write a book and I had felt like a failure for returning to Rutgers. *"Take it easy,"* Richard said, his words still alive and speaking to me who am old enough now to be his father then, *"if I've learned anything from my own experience in this half-assed profession, it's that the best advice any writer can give to another is simply: take it easy and good luck. . . . Don't, in other words, jazz yourself up into a nervous wreck. Be quiet, be as sane as you can, and let the work come out of you. And one final piece of solemn, teacherly advice, and I do mean this: try to like yourself better."*

And that's all, just this letter and the books and the memory of his gentle voice and his tall thin and tabid body, his soft eyes and, as Hemingway once said of Fitzgerald, his almost feminine features. Perhaps he was his generation's Fitzgerald, for he was a much greater writer than I was aware of then. *Revolutionary Road*, as good as it was, didn't quite make it to *Madame Bovary*, but *Easter Parade* would, as if in a scoreboard like the one in Mailer's *Advertisements For Myself*, which was a best seller that spring, it would make the game where it doesn't matter who is better than whom but only that everyone plays, including the benchwarmers if only for a moment.

"Art is a very big place," wrote Paul Fussell in his own letter to me that spring, *"and it includes all kinds as different as*

Ben Jonson and Saroyan." Fussell had been my freshman prof and he was the same age as Richard and Mailer, too old to be older brothers and yet too young to be fathers. As I write about them now I stare at their letters as if at a family album, the used copy of *Easter Parade* like a madeleine in a research of lost times.

For what and for whom were all the books that shored our walls against the emptiness? For the beautiful woman, wrote Mailer when he was young, but what difference would she make when she would stand by his deathbed? No, said the emptiness when I walked back here with Richard's book in my arm, it was all for nothing, all the words and all the coffee like Blake's *abomination of desolation.*

Then back here I opened Richard's book and it started again, the wave up my spine as the words flowed into the dark story of another miserable life. How beautiful they were, how beautiful the miserable Emily who was Richard himself, how beautifully he imagined her out of his pain. Look, look how beautifully he makes her speak, how beautifully he brings to life our desolate America, not since *Ethan Frome* and *Miss Lonelyhearts* has the abomination been so bright and clear, his love of Flaubert like an apple in the tree, I myself reaching to write as well. "Love Genius," Blake said, "it is the face of God."

But why the cigarettes and bourbon, was God but a front man for tobacco and alcohol? Why the misery for the sake of a line, what kind of love was it that shoved a man into a basement and made him want to escape through art? Climb the tree and find the answer, go back to when it first took root.

It all started with Mailer's young woman, or Fame as she was sometimes called, *Fama* in Latin rooted to speech, the photo on the jacket like a hero who would win the Beatrice in the giant rose, no art without ego and yet art itself a letting go.

"Is William Saroyan a great writer?" I once asked my cousin Archie when I began to trade my baseball cards for those in art. "I don't know if he's great or not," said Archie, who was my first hero in the new game, "but a lot of people used to love his stories."

This was at the start of Fifties when Archie himself began his own artisthood by quitting *Hopalong Cassidy* and going to the Art Students League to collect the G.I. Bill. It was Archie who first led me to the tree and fed me with Harold Foster's *Prince Valiant* and then moved on to Picasso before I was ten. When the Fifties started his old army buddy, Avati, was illustrating the Signet pocketbooks of new novels like Ellison's *Invisible Man* and Mailer's *Barbery Shore*. "Look," Archie said when Moravia's *Woman Of Rome* came out, "another cover by Avati."

And who else, what were their names who are now buried in the great compost, the paperbacks like *Woman Of Rome* now shredding at the slightest touch into sprinkles of nothingness? One day Archie said Saroyan had sat at the next table in the *Horn and Hardart Automat* by the League. That's when I asked if Saroyan was a great writer. Every Armenian home had a copy of *My Name Is Aram* with the Don Freeman drawings, and along with my Aunty Askig's big Random House Giant of *Anna Karenina* it became an icon more powerful than any Bible or cross, though I wouldn't read anything but comics until I was thirteen. I was a late reader but a great fan of the abundant films and comics and the radio shows, so by the fourth grade I was already writing my own stories.

Then Archie lent me Somerset Maughm's anthology that included *The Daring Young Man On The Flying Trapeze*, and it had sprouted, the tree that would become a cross of suffering and redemption, the faces of fame like manure for its growth.

Yet there were no faces at first, for those were the days

before a face came with every story or poem however slight, and I didn't know what Saroyan looked like when his lines led to artisthood and shipwreck. How beautiful they were, how beautiful the young man who starved to death for the sake of art, how beautiful his suffering in the face of a venal and profane America. Look, said a love entwined with longing, look how beautifully they reflect the long-ing on a rainy afternoon, my love of genius e n t w i n e d with the need to l o v e myself.

"You too," the Daring Young Man seemed to say, "can be beautiful," then he led to *Martin Eden* in the old twenty-five cent Penguin edition, Martin Eden himself diving from a ship like the Daring Young Man starving to death, or later like Hart Crane in the ecstatic *Voyages* that opened with the *"great wink of eternity,"* his arms wide as he dived into the waves like a flying trapeze or reaching for an apple.

But if the beautiful lines were Saroyan, then who was the gruff old man who opened the door of a tract house in Fresno twenty years later?

"Mr. Saroyan?" "What do you want?" "I . . . uh . . . I just stopped by to uh . . . thank you for the kind letter you sent my publisher about my book. My mother moved near here and I just thought I'd stop by for a minute." "Oh, yes, yes," he said, his gruffness dissolving into his open-hearted innocence, "I remember, come in, come in."

A chaos of printed matter filled the rooms as he led the way to the one in which he was writing, a small black and white flashing images with no sound and some music playing softly on the old phonograph. Then seeing I was shy he went into one of his monologues to fill the silence. Fill the silence, said his own kind of emptiness, fill the rooms with pictures and songs and memoirs and stories, keep making lines even on your deathbed. "Are these drawings by your grandchild?" I said, looking at the scribbles. "No," he said, "they're mine."

And what else from that afternoon with my childhood hero, is there nothing left but an old man living alone with mounds of printed matter like compost and mulch? This is, I thought, what really happens to the daring young writer on the flying trapeze, Jack London dying not in the sea but from too many pills.

Yet their stories were true in art if not in biography, my love for them leading to the library where I was ready for an even deeper thrill. *The Short Stories Of Ernest Hemingway,* said the old Scribner edition in the quiet little branch, the silence and the odor more holy than a church and the aisles like the saints where the nuns prayed from statue to statue behind the monastery, the lines flowing like mantras.

"In the fall the war was always there but we did not go to it anymore," said one of them, Fitzgerald himself quoting this very line in a letter. It was the first sentence of the story, *In Another Country,* and it had electrified me like a guru's feather in my high school textbook, thus making me search for more in the library. How beautiful it was when the sound fused with the meaning which was not really about a young soldier but something deeper. What was it that was deeper than the subject, what was it that caused the wave up my spine? Look, look at how they flow, all the beautiful lines about death.

It was Hemingway's story of his own love of writing that would touch me most, and I would read it for the first time when I returned from the dead in Leninakan, it was not really a story but part of his *Garden Of Eden,* which he may have written around the time I fell in love with him and when he himself was in deep despair, it was the story of a young writer writing about a boy who sees a vision in the form of an elephant. It wouldn't be published until after he had killed himself, for he had locked it away when he thought he couldn't get it up anymore.

Look, he seemed to say, look how beautiful is the act of writing, the young writer waking at dawn to write about a boy who has a vision of an elephant, the writing itself a vision. Look how the words appear like the dawn of awakening, look at the magic of words and how they blossom and fruit, look how wonderful it is to write a story. This is what I truly love, he was saying, this is my garden where I have worked so hard with love and devotion. Then he killed himself as if it were gone, the elephant slaughtered and its ivory sold in what Blake would call *the desolate market.*

Yet there was no market in that quiet library and there was nothing to sell or gain when I first started my own journey, there was just the love of words and it was Hemingway who led the way as he had for others, for he was a boy's writer and his best work was of innocence and love, the bullfighter and the prizefighter and the old guerrillas all seen through the eyes of an innocence that was both horrified and fascinated with death and dying. It was the boy in him who listened to the old whore in a depot and at the sad waiter at closing time, it was the boy who imagined the old fisherman and treasured friendship so deeply. Regarding the make-believe that the marketplace would value, well, as Ezra Pound would write in his prison cage, *"What thou lovest well remains and the rest is dross."*

And I did love it and I wanted to imitate it as if there were an instinct to repeat art like birds weave a nest. I too wanted to write a story and who better to imitate than Hemingway whose formula was so simple and whose persona so heroic? To be a writer I too needed some kind of war to witness suffering and even suffer myself, Hemingway becoming a father figure as he himself needed to be a *"Papa"* to face the emptiness, to be a strong father who could protect a home and make everything well, to be a *man*, for the world could be cruel, especially to artists.

Yet to be a man I had to compete with other men and catch a reader as if the fish of survival. Could I do this, could I cast my line into the sea and eat from the feast of life? One afternoon in high school I suddenly panicked. By now there was no turning back and I panicked at the darkness ahead, the terrible market looming like a dragon. How could I survive with my little lines that would rip and drown in the merciless waves, the fish of life forever gone? No, I would fail, I was no Hemingway or London in a war or Alaska, I had to go to college first, especially since I was so poorly read. I would have to read all those books I should have already by now and I would have to get a degree for some kind of job to pay the rent. It had begun, the fight between the need to write and my other needs in my own kind of war and Alaska. Then came my peers with whom I would learn by competing with, as if in a game where everyone could play as long as we practiced.

Norman Fruchter was the first and most important, his name itself like his talent for fructifying and nurturing. He was a senior when I was a freshman and we worked as shipping clerks in the basement of the University Press, the both of us from the working-class and Rutgers itself in a kind of working-class Ivy League for those who couldn't afford Princeton or Brown. It was then a pleasant little campus and like the classes the Press was in a quaint old house that seemed redolent of the very humanities they were meant to nourish. Upstairs, as if in a cozy home, were the secretaries, Ginny and Joanne, and above them on the second floor, tucked away in her little room like Yates's heroine in *Easter Parade*, was the mysterious assistant editor, Helen, who commuted from her single-woman bohemian pad in Greenwich Village and was rarely ever seen. Then, in the spacious attic with the delicious odor of his pipe tobacco and the photo of his friend, Robert Frost, was the beautiful Mr. Sloane, or Bill, as Norman called him, himself in his fifties then, since he was the same age as the Thomas Wolfe in the story he once told when he came down for one of his rare visits to the basement, the shipping table filled with a new book of poems by Norman's adviser, John Ciardi.

"I was just starting as an editor for my family's publishing house," Bill said standing by the stacks, the old books smelling of dust and the new of shiny covers. "Then one day a young man about my age came in with a manuscript that was at least four feet high! 'Ahem,' I said, 'thank you very much,' and that night I took home a chunk of it. It was powerful but I couldn't imagine going through another three and a half feet, so I turned it down and he took it to Maxwell Perkins over in Scribner's and it became *Look Homeward, Angel.*"

He was a kind and generous soul, William Sloane, and he, like Richard, would die from tobacco and alcohol and the long lonely commute in his *Kharman Ghia* to his post-divorce home in the Catskills, he too devoting his life to words. *"You can use my name as reference if it ever happens to come in handy"* he wrote in another letter I saved from those days. *"You've made a damn good uphill fight thus far and I've got every confidence that you'll continue to do so. Don't forget the picture in my office of the little boat sailing the uphill river. Things are pretty much like that all the way through but there's a lot of good fun in the voyaging as well as the stress and strain."*

There seems now a kind of destiny that led me to the Press and Bill Sloane and the ghost of Thomas Wolfe

whom Norman was eager to purge. "I read all of Wolfe in high school," Norman said, "I thought he was the greatest, but I can't read him anymore." Norman was writing his own novel then and sections of it would appear in the college literary magazine, *Anthologist*, along with artwork by his former roommate, Lucas Samaras. It even had articles by Samaras' mentor, Alan Kaprow, who was a young art professor just beginning to create his *Happenings*, and Kaprow's friends, the sculptor George Segal and the painter Roy Lichtenstein, were working in studios nearby. And in that same magazine were also poems by the great scholar, Francis Fergusson, and by Ciardi who was becoming famous after his Dante translations had just come out.

It was Norman who got that magazine going, just as he would help nurture so many other seeds to fruition, like the film study programs for workingclass kids in London and the political journal *Studies On The Left* and the *Newsreel Collective* in the years to come. He was a fiercely active young man and his passion for politics vied for his time with his love of fiction. Even as an undergrad with papers due and his own novel in progress he found a way to get involved with the local movement for civil rights which had just gained momentum in the south. He would often come to work weary and yet he would always find time to help the freshman who needed to learn as much as he could. "What don't you understand?" he said when I asked him for help with a stanza from a strange poem.

It was from *Sailing To Byzantium* and Paul Fussell had assigned it without title or author in the honors English class. The others in class would have no trouble writing an A paper, but I really didn't belong in the class because it was just for those who got A's in the first semester and I got only a B plus. There were only six of them in the entire freshman class of a thousand, but I had gone to Fussell and asked him to please let me in, I couldn't be held down in the other ordinary classes, even though I was slow. And so he had let me in the little room in the old house across the street from the Press while he stood by the board like a magus.

Like Yates he was still unknown then, but he too was in love with writing and had devoted his life to it. In personality he was like Kenneth Clark, the author of *The Nude* which had just appeared in paperback with the cover designed by Leonard Baskin, and he even looked a little like Clark, though more glamorous with his shiny blond hair and even features. He would always be on time and he would slip his little gold watch from the slit of the pocket just under his belt and set it on the table with his pack of *Parliaments* from which he would smoke three and only three filtered cigarettes, one in the beginning of class, one exactly in the middle and one at the end. He was the exact type, precise and punctual and as perfect in his dress as in the clear and even penmanship that would in the margins of our weekly papers prick any balloons of sloppy logic and excessive paragraphs, his voice commanding us to be true and clear as if he were Michelangelo's Pantocrator in the *Last Judgement*.

Why, what difference did it make? Because, said his own love of writing, imagination needs reason to give form to vision, and he would help us clear the windows of our minds. And so in that cozy little room that had been a kitchen or a drawing room of a family long ago, we looked up at the board as a lyric appeared in crisp letters like what Blake would call a *window into eden*. Look, said Fussell's love, can you see how beautiful it is? Yes, it was beautiful, but what did it mean?

You will understand what it means later, said his gentle patience, for under the stern appearance he was not a ruthless taskmaster, yet who was the mysterious professor who looked as if he was standing in Windsor Castle to have tea with T.S. Eliot? One day he alluded to his soldier days and that was all we would ever know of them until twenty years later when we would read his deeply moving books, *The Great War and Modern Memory* and *Doing Battle*.

"A man doesn't really understand a book until he has lived at least a part of it," said Pound's *ABC Of Reading*, which had just come out in paperback by a new publisher, New Directions, Pound himself also of a pedagogical type. It was Pound's recently published *Pisan Cantos* that Fussell had assigned to me when each of us had to report on the critical reception of a controversial book. It was the most difficult book and I was the least capable of understanding it, my much smarter classmate, Pinsky, getting *God and Man At Yale*. I was supposed to get *Lolita*, but it had just been banned, so Fussell gave me the late Cantos instead, and it was in them that I first read *"What thou lovest well remains, the rest is dross,"* its cadence, like the lines of Yeats and Hemingway, remaining through the years like a mantra, though its deeper meaning would not appear until my middle age.

Meanwhile, back in the shipping basement with Norman, I had handed him the mimeograph of the stanza that began with *"An aged man is but a paltry thing. . . ."*
"Who wrote it?" I asked Norman. "It doesn't matter," he said, "just read it as if if he's speaking to you and tell me what you don't understand."

"An aged man is but a paltry thing," I read aloud, *"a tattered coat upon a stick, unless soul clap its hands and sing, and louder sing for every tatter in its mortal dress. Nor is there singing school but studying monuments of its own magnificence. And therefore I have sailed the seas and come to the holy city of Byzantium."*

"What don't you understand?" Norman said. " 'Nor is there singing school but studying,' " I said, "what does that mean?" "What do you think it means?" he said. "I don't know," I said. "Comon," he said, "don't play that game."

And so Norman, who was only twenty-one himself, guided me through the line like an older brother who was learning it as well, the basement in the meantime filled with stacks of Ciardi's new book, *As If*, and John Higham's *Strangers In A Strange Land* and Peter Charanis' *A History of Byzantium*.

And is there now, in the great void to whom this memoir is addressed, anyone reading this who knows of the historians, John Higham and Peter Charanis, or of Norm Fruchter himself whose first novel would be called *A Coat Upon A Stick?* The last would appear in the mail two years later with its white jacket glowing like a magic egg in the straw-filled wrapper from Spottiswoode, Ltd. in London. Norman would move to London after he got a Fulbright to study Shakespeare. He had applied for a Rhodes Scholarship but they gave it to a Peter something like Dawkins or Watkins who was a star quarterback for Princeton, so Norman took the Fulbright instead. He was writing the first draft of the novel before he left. He was using Ginny's typewriter in the Press where he could be alone and not in the pad he shared with Bill Belli on the other side of New Brunswick. Bill Sloane let him have the key and he would sit with the big Underwood in the office late at night and type intensely with one finger like a woodpecker on the tree of life, Norman the Genius whom I loved with that kind of love young men have for more talented peers, he was the first of the many who would keep appearing through the years.

It was a powerful spring in that year of '59, so full of books and people like new buds on the great tree that would keep growing and shedding, each day packed with the Press and the classes and the weary evenings in the library, all to be an artist and win the prize, the young woman who would accompany happiness.

"Picasso always had a woman in his life and his work," said Kaprow in that Friday morning class that was only for seniors. "Just come," Norman had said to me, "Allen won't mind."

It was a special treat sitting in on that Picasso class with the small select group of seniors, the young Kaprow looking old and wise with his beard and artist compromise of denim workshirt and tie, his voice both hip and academic as he talked about how the collages were created in a modern way where everything could fit together, his fellow artist George Segal creating on the other side of town the white sculptures that would want to link the living and dead.

In the meantime, back in Fussell's class, I continued competing and learning with my new friends, Pinsky and Henry Dumas who would become poets and Bob Maniquis a professor of comp lit and Ernie Ruckle a dramatist and Kenny Gorelick a psychiatrist and Jimmy Hughes a history

prof. And I, what would I become, sitting here worrying as usual about how I'll pay the rent now that the unemployment checks have stopped?

One of our textbooks was the new fifty cent Dell pocketbook anthology edited by Robert Penn Warren and Albert Erskine, *Six Centuries of Great Poetry From Chaucer To Yeats*, the strange name of Chidiock Tichborne inserted between them. Who in God's name was Chidiock Tichborne, "born? and died 1586"? There was only one poem by him, called *Elegy*, but the editors didn't mention that he too was only eighteen when he was beheaded in the Tower Of London, his poem written in one of the cells and its refrain like another mantra, *And now I live and now my life is done.*

Such a strange and moving poem and even more moving than had it been by someone anonymous. For anonymous, like whoever wrote the great *Western Wind*, meant that he or she was some genius whose name didn't matter anymore, but Chidiock Tichborne was not anonymous, he was Chidiock Tichborne whom no one knew except Robert Penn Warren and Albert Erskine, his very name like a joke. How could anyone exist with such a name, and yet his poem was included where others were not and he had made the Big Game after all, there was hope after all, even for someone like me, who really did not belong in the honors class.

But the competition would be fierce and merciless, the beautiful woman waiting in the castle like a female for the strongest male, the survival of the fittest not really with others but myself. Then one week we were assigned instead of a paper on a poem a poem itself. "This week you're to write a poem yourself," said Fussell, "and let's see if you find it any easier."

And so we returned to our dorms to do the best we could, but what did best mean and what really was a poem? For weeks we had written about what it meant in order to prove our intelligence, yet a poem was not proving intelligence, it was not proving anything, and we went back to our rooms as if to the great court itself, Fussell the coach who would decide if we had made the team or not, I the only one really desperate about the challenge, the others each confident that they were the most verbally intelligent and could write whatever they wanted. Then said Fussell in the following week, "Well, out of these seven poems only one shows the mark of a creative writer."

Alas, I had cleared the first hurdle, for had I not cleared it perhaps I would have left the race to become a normal person for the rest of my life, but no, I cleared it and the following hurdles would tumble much later when it would be too late to start again, the others moving on successfully regardless of what Fussell had said, Pinsky poems actually appearing in the Norton Anthology itself and Dumas' read by young Blacks all over the country after he was martyred by a cop in a Harlem subway.

If Pinsky was annoyed by Fussell's comment he didn't say so afterwards, and with his usual confidence he shrugged it away. He was sure he could write good poems and did indeed want very much to be a good poet, for he loved poetry as much as anyone. If this memoir were fiction he could easily at eighteen be transformed into a character who would say something like, "I have no time for anything else beside becoming a poet."

But he also wanted to be happy, for like most of us, he was an unhappy young man, not as tormented as I but almost as gloomy sometimes when still in his pajamas by mid-afternoon he sipped *Mr. Boston's Gin* instead of getting laid. Most eighteen year old freshmen didn't get laid in those days, and maybe don't nowadays either, the only ones who got laid were the older married guys like Dumas and the successful Romeos like Maniquis. It was one of the great human wounds that in the prime of our juices we would be poisoned by ungratified desire and masturbate shamefully in library toilets, our flesh knotted in pain when it was most ripe for commingling. Some like me would carry that wound for the rest of our lives and struggle to heal it, others like Pinsky would be more fortunate and heal themselves earlier. It was no surprise that by senior year he was married to a lovely young woman from across the river in Douglas. Almost everyone who met him was attracted to his warm smile and charming humor, his working-class roots enriched by a quick mind that put him at ease with anyone from a day laborer to a Fussell. Like many of us he had been educationally deprived in the public schools and he would, said ambitious youth, have to work hard to complete the reading list every poet needed to be great.

"Beware of this, O ambitious youth," Melville would say years later when we were ready to understand *Moby Dick*, *"all mortal greatness is but disease."* Yet to undergrads in love with greatness and hungry for learning, these words would have to wait. At the end of that freshman year Fussell invited us to his home in the University Heights for a goodbye party. He supported his wife and kids on a small salary, but though his home was modest it was tasteful and we felt honored to be invited there. It was clear by now that he had a teacher's love for us, but it would take a lifetime before we would know that kind of love ourselves, the love for youth and the force of life through its limbs. In reading his books years later and learning of his hatred for war, it would seem that his love was related to his own friends who died beside him on a battlefield when they were so young themselves. Perhaps we reminded him of that love as we sat in his living room safe and alive.

In the memory of him serving us pretzels and drinks, I now feel like a veteran myself from another kind of battlefield, our youth so innocent as we embarked on our different journeys. How could he help but love us when we were so hungry to suckle from his mind? It was at that party

he mentioned what he thought were the five most impor-
tant novels in the twentieth century, *Ulysses, The Magic
Mountain, The Counterfeiters, The Sound And The Fury,* and
Remembrance Of Things Past.

Pinsky would read the first four the following semesters
and the last before he left for Stanford. He even read *Ulysses*
without the Stuart Gilbert guide, as if it were just another
novel which as well as being a great narrative poem it actually is. He was endowed with the gift of reading well like a
professional athlete with a physical ability, but of course
neither would succeed without love and striving. He loved
to read the way some boys love a basketball so deeply they
sleep with it, and as a child he once gobbled the words on a
cereal box as if they were as essential to his life as the food
inside. I would lose touch with him after he disappeared
into high achievement, but I can still see him lying in bed
all morning and turning pages as if he were eating *Wheaties,
Breakfast of Champions.* Like John Ciardi in those days, he's
now working on his own translation of *The Divine Comedy,*
or so said Alan a few weeks ago. But he doesn't know Italian,
I said. He learned it, Alan said. But why *The Divine Comedy,*
I wondered, did it have something to do with Fergusson?

Norman was the first to mention Fergusson, and
Fussell himself recommended him highly. But he gave only
two classes a semester and they quickly filled, perhaps
partly because he gave nothing lower than a B, and if we
didn't complete the reading it wouldn't matter because he
would have everyone read aloud in class as if we were in
kindergarten. He could do whatever he wanted because he
was a full professor and he was the whole comp lit department by himself after it was created especially for him,
none of the other departments wanting him because, said
the gossip, he had only a B.A. and didn't play by their rules.
It may have even been the university president himself,
Mason Gross, who created the chair to bring Francis to

Rutgers. His *Idea Of A Theatre* was a major work, a wise and profound book in simple and genial prose, and so too his *Dante's Drama Of The Mind* and his introduction to *Aristotle's Poetics*, all now out of print and only old geezers like myself aware of them.

He was given a tiny room in the back corner of the little old German Department house and there in his humble space he sat like a monk in a mountain cave in his weekly office hours, in case anyone would climb the creaky stairs to visit him. Many of us were too shy and so he was alone most of the time, but one all too very quiet afternoon, the stairs did creak with fearful sneakers when I climbed as softly as I could, then as I turned the banister there he was sitting behind his desk looking eager and waving a happy welcome as if I were a gift. "Come in, come in," he said with his eyebrows rising, "it's good to see you."

Did he really mean that, I wondered, so good for a wise old man to see such a young fool? He seemed so sincere and friendly and not until now, myself the same age which I dread to call old, would I understand how happy mine or

anyone's visit had made him. His wife had recently died and he was living alone somewhere near Princeton. "Sit down, sit down," he said, "of course I would be very happy to read your story."

His own youth was supposed to have been wild during the twenties in Paris, and he himself once told us in class the anecdote of how he was so haughty he missed meeting James Joyce. *Ulysses* had just been published and he had been invited to a party where he could meet the famous author, but he wouldn't go to a party just to meet someone famous, who cared about meeting some James Joyce anyway? "I'll always regret that," he said, his gentle voice softened by age.

It is his voice and his big hands and his vibrant thespian eyes that are now etched in my memory like a Rembrandt, the light slanting through the window on his face as he sat behind his desk like the lost father come home again, his lips reciting like a song the beautiful rhythm of the original Greek for Joyce's *wine dark sea*. It was a voice like the sea itself when small waves hush upon a quiet shore, and it seemed not only his but an eternal voice as if he were a kind of guru, it was beautiful even when he recited in Italian the lines from the *Inferno* that rendered the sound of teeth gnawing a skull with vengeance, it was the voice of the *mimesis* he introduced with the *Poetics* and it was about how out of nothing but breath a living form could flow around the world like radio waves that never disappear. Listen, he seemed to say, and you will hear the eternal voice made manifest through art.

"Now what is the action here?" he would ask after each of us read aloud a passage from a great tragedy about being human. What did he mean? I kept wondering, and he kept asking the same question as if it were a koan I still keep asking myself. What is tragedy, what is art, what is the motive in our journey through life, *what*, as Blake's Enion would cry, *is the price of experience?*

Perhaps it would have been better to have reserved such questions for older students more capable of understanding them, perhaps such teaching is wasted on youth who needing food and shelter might be better off learning something mechanical, just as young art students would benefit more from learning computers than to be led into the perilous waters of creation so quickly. Perhaps it is true that art is not for everyone and anyone daring to fly its trapeze without a way to pay the rent will be doomed to a crippling fall. Perhaps literature and art departments serve only to salary professors like Fussell and Fergusson who never warn how the love of art can lead to social misery. Better for a young man to learn how to repair a car than what moves the soul, some parents now paying twice my yearly income just to nurture in their children a love of art and a future of minimum wage. Perhaps art should be only for a select few as in the ages of pyramids and slaves.

Yet the memory is still vivid of an old man not really old who kept asking what moves the soul and leads to catharsis. I would keep in touch with him over the years, and he would reply with little notes whose penmanship grew weaker until the last was almost illegible, then came the note from his second wife, Peggy. He was always happy to get my letters, she said, but crippled by Parkinson's he had to apologize for not answering them. Then came her note saying he had died. I had seen the effects of that disease in my cousin, Edna, and I shuddered at the thought of Francis dying the same way.

"Now what is the action here," he would ask, then he would wait patiently for someone to reply. Pinsky, sitting next to me, had with his quickness no trouble finding at least an academic answer, and once with noblesse oblige he even passed it to me on a slip of paper. In fact he learned so well he would say years later that he "sometimes felt sheepish" about getting paid so highly for lecturing on what he learned from Francis Fergusson when he was only twenty.

Pinsky and I shared an apartment in the fall semester of our senior year and it was then I invited both the widower Fergusson and Fussell to one of our parties. The apartment was the first floor of a small old clapboard duplex at 58 Stone Street just a few blocks from campus, and we got it from Steve Vasey, a young art student who had painted the walls with rebellious blacks and oranges as if they were works by Rothko and Kline, the little rooms more like one of Kaprow's *Happenings* than a home, *Typical Young Artists' Pad With Old Stove That Hasn't Been Cleaned For Generations.*

Step right in, said the doors which were always open in those days, here is the launching pad of more young men who will like Stephen Daedalus *go to encounter for the millionth time the reality of experience.*

"We should buy a hundred pound sack of potatoes and keep it in the basement," Pinsky had suggested when we moved in. Since we both enjoyed potatoes it would be cheap and filling and we wouldn't be bothered with shopping. So we ate a lot of potatoes that semester and we each typed in our separate rooms as if launching our ships to our different destinies of green or desert islands, our party now scumbling into a fantasy of bigger one and the steps leading up to our pad like a ladder into an apple tree, everyone glowing in the long rays of a late autumn twilight, *the young in one another's arms, commending all summer long, whatever is begotten, born, and dies.*

There by our typewriters and old mattresses are Fussell and Fergusson and even Richard Yates, who actually did come to another party after reading on campus on his way to Washington to speechwrite for Bobby Kennedy. And with him, why not, since this is a vision party, is my cousin Archie down from Woodstock, and what the heck, Leo

Litwak as well which could have been possible since he was in Manhattan in those days, and dear Sam Astrachan, who was then living in uptown Manhattan though like Leo he wouldn't become a friend until many years later. And Alan is here and Norman and even Fred Tremallo, that passionate young writer who later became a dean at Phillips Exeter, and Jim Mohan, who was no less passionate and later the headmaster of a girls elementary school in San Francisco. And good old Bobby Schectman of course, that great jazz trombonist who lived around the corner on Prosper Street, and with him dear Jack Ruhlman who was to become a great Blake man and cartoonist. Even the painter Lenny Silverberg has come by bus from Manhattan where he was just a young fauve in the East Village, though he had not yet heard of the crazy Armenian in New Brunswick. And arriving on that same bus is Gatz Hjortsberg down from Dartmouth and even the poets Bob Hass and Gerry Wilson flying in from California and England and the dramatist Daniel Rudman and the screenwriter Henry Bean, though Daniel and Henry were only in high school then, all my friends and fellow artists are here in my party of artisthood and everyone else in love with art is welcome as well.

And there should be women too of course, though art was hard for them in those days, unlike later when they would easily defeat an old Caucasian male for teaching jobs. But Jennifer Haring has come because she was ahead of her time when she left Douglas to live in the Village and write pornography to pay her rent while she worked on her novel. Good old Bill Belli, now a lawyer in Nevada, tried to put the make on her that autumn and he is here too like a young Boswell just back from Paris with exotic stories of his new friends, Jim Jones and Bill Burroughs and Jimmy Baldwin. Of course Hank Dumas is here, for he actually shared that apartment after Pinsky got married. And here is also Hank Heifetz who of all my friends would influence me most. He was just back from Italy then and living on Spring Street in Manhattan, the next thirty years facing him with the hardship that comes when genius is unrecognized, his great versions of Kalidasa and Kampan read only by cognoscenti.

They are all here now, all my friends in art when we shared books and potatoes, all those who know what it's like to look out the window to the apple tree. Look now, says the window as if it is the young woman who was to be the prize. She is Persephone now, picking flowers for her future husband like a graduate student researching a party of bon voyage, an old Fergusson the toastmaster with the bottle of bourbon he had brought that night, his love of books breaking it on the bow to the Great Library of The Void, the Young Artists raising their cups for their places on the shelves. How eager they are, she notes, how hungry and hopeful. To art! they shout as they embark, their books carried from pad to pad and job to job so they could each sit by their separate windows.

But it would get harder and harder as the jobs dried up and the pads became gentrified. Some would fare well in academia or Hollywood, but others would shipwreck and send their work like floating bottles.

Don't give up, the ghost of Hank Dumas would say, his tall thin figure like a Malcolm X.

Don't forget the little boat sailing the uphill river, the ghost of Bill Sloane would say with the picture in his office.

Find another job, the ghost of Richard would say in between the lines of his letter, *you need a job to keep writing.*

What for? despair would ask, *what for when it always fails?*

For eternity, Blake would answer, *for Eden.*

It fails, a failure would repeat, the bare tree now empty of fruit and about to be cut by a new landlord, *it is like that little boat I made in kindergarten and sailed in a sewer because there was no other water. I dropped it through the bars but the string was too short and it disappeared into the blackness, it was my artisthood and it left me stranded.*

It went to the sea, would say the little boy who cut his finger sawing the wood, *it is waiting for you at the pier.*

WINDOW INTO EDEN

"Whenever you're miserable," an old mother once said, "be around young people and they will make you happy."

Sometime later a ball hit a sub in the back of the head in a gym class at Westlake Junior High. "Who threw that ball!" yelled the fool who realized even before he finished his question how stupid it was. At least he didn't get hit in the nose with a book like another sub and or have his hat stolen.

"We love to dump on subs," one kid explained in a more peaceful moment.

"Yeh, I know, I was kid once too."

"Where was that?"

"West Hoboken, New Jersey."

"Oh, New Jersey, I heard a dat place."

"You know where it is?"

"Not really. Is it near Chicago? My uncle lives in Chicago."

And so there was a chance to entertain them with a little geography for a few minutes before their hormones went wild again. That was in the spring, but it's summer now and an old dauber has returned to his lines by his little window, the past semester in retrospect with all those kids his mother said would make him happy. *"Oh woe is me!"* he cried last winter when there was no other way to pay the rent, "is this what I have come to?" Then the phone would ring at five a.m. and the computer voice would say, "We have a substitute position available, to accept press one, to decline. . . ."

It wouldn't have been so bad with five hours sleep, but waking in the dark night of the soul at three a.m., he would have to plod through another day of outrageous fortune and erasers. *"Well, what did you expect?"* said the ghost of Aunty Manooshag who had warned about artisthood, *"you could have been a regular school teacher who would be retired by now."*

But were there no other jobs like those so plentiful in the Sixties, and after all the years as a migrant lecturer was there not one little class some merciful college could throw like a bone? No, said the Nineties, you can't compete anymore and the hard rain has started to fall. Then, as in the Stones song that said we may not get what we want but if we try sometimes we get what we need, along came the

Oakland Public School District with $92.50 a day, but not the Berkeley District that had enough subs with long vitas, no, Berkeley was no longer for refugees from the marketplace.

In the Berkeley of the olden days, however, there was once a run with Peter Stine and John Ruhlman in the hills above Strawberry Canyon, the future looming with a New Age and each of them writing theses on modern literature and Blake. Then a quarter century later the phone rang from Ann Arbor and Peter, now the editor of a magazine called *Witness*, said, "I'm putting together an issue on cities and John told me you're subbing in Oakland, do you think you can write something about it?"

Oakland, the land of the live-oaks, some of which still stood in the sprawl from the bay to the hills, the city in history suddenly alive in the Montera schoolyard with a pubescent girl yelling at a boy, "Shut up or I'll put my crotch in your face!" Her voice was a reveille to an old sub who sat daydreaming about the light on a tree. Here was reality, said her voice as she walked away mumbling something about her "kootchy hole" he would never hear were he back in his cottage struggling with composition.

Montera was in the Oakland hills where the rich lived, and it was supposed to be a better junior high than the others. "Do you live around here?" the sub asked one of the boys who was sitting alone and was now supposed to check "Afro-American" instead of a "black" for identity. Whatever happened to "black is beautiful," thought the sub as he looked lovingly at the boy's face, a dark skin so much richer in pigment than a light one, why not be free of Africa and Armenia and the suffering of selfhood? *"We need to give our children an identity they can be proud of,"* some had said, ignoring the wars. "We are all Africans," said a poster along the halls. No, the boy said, he didn't live in the hills, he lived in East Oakland, but his mother gave a different address so he wouldn't have to go to a school there, then he mentioned that he actually was Afro-American, since his absent father was Nigerian.

Then one day in Lazear Elementary on 29th Avenue, the sixth grade was Spanish-speaking, and on the field for Cinco de Mayo the kids seemed to enjoy being Latino together, their little school of humble huts like an oasis amid the abandoned factories and noisy freeway. How lovely their togetherness appeared, yet could there be an identity that would include everyone?

"We can call each other 'nigger' " a seventh grader said in Lowell Middle School one afternoon, "but if a white person say it we be angry."

He kept yelling the word at his friends in the same way Armenian boys in Yerevan would yell "Hye-deghah!" which meant "Armenian boy!"

"In the Sixties we struggled to be free of that word," the vice-principal had said when he heard the yelling, "and I don't want to hear it anymore!" But after he left the boy and his pals yelled it again and pushed each other as if this were the only way they knew to show affection, the girls nearby playing beauty parlor by tying their hair in whatever they were now called that used to be called pigtails. Then one of the noisy boys came to the desk and mumbled a West Oakland accent too slurred for a West Hobokener to understand the first time. "He threw my comb out the window," he repeated.

His thick curly hair was cut so close it could have been a five o'clock shadow and why he needed a comb was a mystery, but at least he'd be gone for a few minutes. "All right, here's another pass, go down and get it and take your time coming back."

Meanwhile the Cambodian, Laotian, Vietnamese, Mexican and Guatemalan kids segregated themselves at the third corner of the room, the two Ethiopian boys, one of whom was actually Eritrean, at the other corner. The Cambodian girls said they were actually born in Thailand where their parents escaped during the massacres of the Khymer Rouge.

"You old," said one of the boys yelling "nigger," his name to be forgotten though his words would be etched deeply in an old brain, "you gonna die."

"How old you?" asked one of his pals.

"Ha!" they laughed when answered.

"How much you pay fo dem?" asked their fashion expert pointing to the *Birkenstocks* which were so worn they looked like they were from Auchswitz.

"Ha!" they laughed again, "we can get them for twenty in *Payless*."

What elementary schools did they go to, asked the sub, and when they said Cole and King where he had subbed before there came the warm feeling of knowing them since they were small and b e i n g part of their

MICHELLE DONSHE
OAKLAND TECH
9/27/96

world, everyone an immigrant to the new age of strange names like his own had been when he was a kid.

"Nisa, Xochil, Aesha, Kaiz," said a typical roll sheet in King Estates one day, "Kamesha, Dartanyan, Sumiko, Roshawn, Jacquice, Iman, Destony, Landous, Eranica, Donshea, Hoai, Michiko, Syreeta, Kim-Ngan, Marquz, Theron, Sala, Jumarri," and so forth.

"My name is Sherena," one girl said. "You never heard that name before 'cause it's a made-up name. It be pretty, ain't it?"

She wanted love, everyone wanted to be someone with love.

She moved near the boys yelling "nigger" while they slammed dominoes like firecrackers, her pal by the desk saying, "The biggest gang be the Mexican Mafia, they kill everyone down to yo dog, you don wanna mess wit the Mexican Mafia, I'm goin where dare black people."

Her skin was light and she could have checked "caucasian" on any form, but she wanted to identify with those who had been her family. Perhaps peace would come with a miscegenation uniting all Capulets and Montagues, for wasn't that the meaning of the true and visionary America?

She was Juliet's age, the age of Dante's Beatrice and Gauguin's *Nevermore* and Degas' dancers who were the poor girls of the street. She was the age an old mother was a servant in Beirut after orphaned by a genocide, the age when Aunty Manooshag was abducted by a Chechen tribe and when old Khatun who just died in a nursing home was a sexual slave before she escaped, she was the age of all the others from the Italy and Ireland which became Vietnam and Salvador. She was history and everyone was a part of it except the old sub who had felt alien and turned to art for refuge, though it was no refuge at all, for art, as Hemingway said, was "at best a lonely life" where an artist "does his work alone and if he is good enough he must face eternity or the lack of it each day."

She was everywhere in all the schools in male and female form and sometimes she was so beautiful she seemed unreal. One quiet and studious morning she was a thirteen year old Asian African Latino and Caucausian who glowed in the nacred light as if she were eternal, the old sub with three hours sleep unable to keep from staring and rubbing his eyes. Was she the one who was raped and mutilated in the news every morning? What sickness hungered for her twilight realm so far away, what was the beast that would send her to the underworld? Something to do with her innocence and the longing for her glow.

JESSICA CANO
OAKLAND '95

Then sex came in the picture as she turned to seduce a boy nearby, her smile in montage with the Montera girl who threatened to put her crotch in a face. The class was supposed to be reading a tale about a Chinese princess with a nightingale, but they all confided to the sub that it was boring. "Then why don't you tell this to your teacher?" he asked. "We don't want to hurt her feelings," one of them said, "she likes it." Then when asked what they would rather read, one of boys recommended a book about the mutilations of a serial killer.

The morning fog dissolved in the noon sun and they poured into the lunchyard like Yeats' *"mackeral crowded sea."* It was no place for an old *"coat upon a stick,"* and the sub stood back to sketch it instead. Come, they said, come join us, come be our sub. Is this your jacket? Let us steal it for a day. Don't be upset, you'll find it across the yard tomorrow morning. We'll teach you what life is all about.

One afternoon in a room without windows in Carter Middle School, they were like prisoners of an insane society. Unable to control them he sat at his desk as if on a death bed, while they turned the room into Vigo's *Zero de Conduite* where the pillows explode into feathers. It was civilization run amuck, from the Malay *amok*, which meant furious attack. Then one of the boys came up to the desk as if to inflict a *coup de grace*.

He had been a screaming banshee all period, but he stood very quietly now and said, "May I have a pass to the bathroom?"

The sub looked at his face as if it were a moment of truth, the banshee suddenly gone and in its place an emissary from enlightenment. He was so beautiful he turned the exhausted sub into an old Mr. Puccatino who had been the janitor down in the basement of Hudson Grammar School where an Armenian kid once ran amuck, the old janitor smoking his pipe and sitting in his rocking chair with the cat curled in his lap and the basement boiler like the Heart of Being that kept everyone warm while snow curtained the windowpanes.

"What did you say?" said the sub to the little angel.

"I said," said the boy, "Can I have a pass to the bathroom?"

No answer came from the defeated sub who sat staring and smiling at someone's darling child.

"Why are you smiling?" the boy asked with embarrassment.

Still no answer, the sub just sitting in the eye of storm like an old Puccatino and the boy glowing like one of Blake's windows into eden.

"Can I please have a pass to the bathroom?" said the boy, confused.

"Here, here's your pass," said the sub, still smiling.

Then the boy left as if to escape the smiling and the love behind it, eager to become a banshee again.

There was nothing to do but love them, for no room without windows or world without vision could keep them from the sickness in the news. Yet how difficult it was to love them when they screamed like banshees and pushed each other instead of hugging and holding hands, when like that boy in
Westlake they threw bottles
and littered a hallway with
broken glass, or like that
second-grader in King
who urinated on the
door after he had
to stand outside
because he was
so wild. How
difficult for
love to grow in a
world of broken
glass and urine
and gunshots on
the street, the dis-
missal delayed until
the police assured
the principal it
was safe.

NAGIA M. DOMBRIAN
KAISER ELEM.
12/5/96

Yet how easy in a calm light like the one in a Degas' paintings where the poor street girls were transformed into angels in ballet, a natural light in rooms with windows instead of the gas tubes of a sickness.

"What happened to the lights?" asked one of the juniors in Skyline High when he entered the room, the sub having shut them so the morning would bathe them in glowing shadows and then raised the blinds raised to the conifers outside.

Then the boy turned the lights on and everyone froze in its painful glare like Daphne into hardness, the glow gone and more profit for Pacific Gas And Electric.

"The sub doesn't like 'em," a girl explained.

"I don't like them either," said another.

"Yeh, me neither."

"Shut 'em off."

"All right, all right," the boy said, and he shut them again, "it just feels so goofy in here with them off."

"Leave 'em off," said a girl busy with her nails, "it feels like school with them on."

"Sure," he said, "I'm just going to sleep anyway."

The glow returned to their lovely faces, the next fifty minutes free of blinds and what Rousseau had called, "the sorry nonsense that goes by the name of education."

Skyline was in the hills and it was supposed to be the best high in the city, the faculty at lunch gossiping about an alumnus, Tom Hanks, who had just won an Academy Award, the lunchroom surrounded by trees like an alpine resort and so different from the ugly one in McClymonds, the alma mater of the basketball pro, Bill Russell.

In the same city where Skyline nestled in the hills like the rich in securities, McClymonds lay forlorn like the poor with scary hallways, a much different school from the one where Russell went. As usual most of the students were absent in the science classes that day, yet the third floor room had a Rubens portrait of Galileo and big windows with a great landscape of the hills in the distance, the sidereal leaves of a tall palm tree looking down on the desolation like a giant star of hope.

Then came a visitor from the local health center with a lecture on the current plagues. She was an attractive woman in her twenties with an East African Muslim name and a degree in Health Sciences from San Francisco State, the kids attentive as she unwrapped condoms and slipped two fingers in and out.

"Some people use oils with these," she said, "like *Vaseline* or *Crisco* or motor oil. . . ."

"Motor oil?" a boy asked amid the laughter.

It was their favorite subject and what they had in common with the universe.

"That's about the size of one of those hats a muslim puts on his head," the boy said regarding a diaphragm.

"Dey got a whole lotta stuff to prevent things happenin," one girl said in regard to a female condom and an I.U.D.

Outside on San Pablo Avenue stood the hookers and addicts like despair itself. Why resist, why struggle, why not die in one of the flophouses by the Greyhound Station and never try to reach the glow, each failure more and more painful?

"It's easy to talk about suicide," an old mother once said regarding a friend in a nursing home, "but how can you kill yourself when your soul is so sweet?" Yet where was the soul so far away like a West Hoboken of a golden age, Mr. Puccatino long gone like rooms of natural light and evergreen oaks?

Was it at Highland Elementary that was supposed to be one of the worst, the gangs no longer like the one in Hudson schoolyard where the boys fought with fists instead of pistols?

A few months before there had been an article in the *East Bay Express* about how bad Highland was, and on the drive out there the sub expected trouble. *What am I doing,* he moaned to the freeway traffic, *wasting my life for a menial wage instead of nurturing it with art?* What the article said seemed true at first, the chainlink campus like a prison where no birds sang on a golden bough, yet what art could blossom without *roots in excrement,* what Eden could flower without the rot of a wasteland? Come, said Highland, come taste the miracle of life not for a menial wage but for your soul.

Then in one of the little huts of kindergarten and first grade, the absent teacher, Mrs. Herman, had created, like her avatar, Mrs. Grotheuseun, once did in West Hoboken, a mini-Eden of storybooks and crayons, and lo and behold, even a little toilet for a caffeine bladder that had to keep pissing.

Yet as always before entering paradise, there was the usual fear and doubt. Were these little cherubs going to fight and scream like those in King where the boy pissed on the door while the principal prepared an assembly on "conflict resolution?" Would these be the children of parents who screamed and teachers who screamed and everyone who screamed on the screen and pulpit the wrath and rules of a paradise lost and unredeemable, were they going to be like that wild little West Hoboken boy himself who screamed and fought his own way out of the golden age? Would these be children like the morning news about child slaves and parents who sold them to reduce their debts, the maw of history like Goya's Saturn eating them one by one? Or would this be, like paradise regained, the little kids' garden where the reincarnation of Mrs. Grotheusen had created a little ark for the voyage home?

Unlike other teachers who left poor lesson plans, Mrs. Herman had the two days designed like a careful tapestry, and the morning begun with a masterpiece called *The Mountain That Loved A Bird*, by Alice McLerran and Eric Carle.

Look, said the love of pictures and words, the old sub himself like the lonely mountain surrounded by the children he had always wanted, look through a vision washed clean of hunger and a history of longing, look through the window to Eden in the story of an old mountain who was always alone until a bird of joy flew into the dark night of his soul.

"Must you leave," the mountain said, "couldn't you just stay here?"

"No," she said (like a woman once said to Old Birkenstocks) she needed food and water and there was none on its bare stone.

And the cherubs looked up at the old sub who was that *mountain made of bare stone . . . alone in a desert plain. . . .*

Look, he said, look how good it feels to be here telling you the story of my soul, and their rapt attention answered like the bird, *"No mountain has ever cared before whether I came or went, and so I will make you a promise since my life will not last forever, I will give to one of my daughters my own name, Joy, and tell her how to find you. And she will have a daughter also and tell her how to find you. . . ."*

But the mountain (like the sub) was not satisfied, he wanted joy forever, until one year, after watching so many daughters come and go, its heart suddenly broke and the hard stone cracked and from its deepest part the tears gushed and rolled down in a stream and the stream watered the stone where joy could tuck a seed into the crack and the seed would grow into a tree where she could finally make her nest and stay.

The little room glowed even in the electric light, but they wanted more, they were not satisfied either, they were not only cherubs but appetites.

Kiss the joy as it flies, reminded Blake, *and live in eternity's sunrise.*

Like hummingbirds they had to keep active and only love could feed their wings with crayons and markers until they were ready to face their own history.

It was that room of love that made them different from the chaos at other schools, the room like a mind which Milton's Satan like an old sub said, *"is its own place, and in itself can make a heaven of hell and hell of heaven."*

And so in the desolation of East Oakland the morning filled with love and more love in the form of coloring and singing, and not only singing *but studying its own magnificence.*

Then came lunchtime and the pleasure of watching them nibble the slaughtered fish and peaches after their uncles and aunts had starved just a decade before. They had survived, they had made it to a garden in East Oakland, and after the kindergartners went home there were just the ten first graders left, the Cambodians, Sameon, Rathanak, Bunthan, Amy Pen, Brenda Sieng, Johnson Cheam, and Buntha and Bunthorn who were twins, and the Latinos, Megan Paez and Hugo Diaz, their names recorded in a journal like the group snapshot Mrs. Herman taped on the wall for a memento jubilare, their faces to fade like *the bird of joy, its wings like feathered fans against the sun.*

They were named to be remembered like that little boat the old sub once made in Mrs. Grotheusen's garden and lost when he tried to sail it, the string slipping down the sewer of the ancient city where there were no streams or ponds. That boat was his soul lost in the underworld like a Persephone, and his old age had become like an old mountain who begged her to return and have daughters in his loneliness. Here now in his little cottage with his lines in the window of an old *Mac*, he searches to open it for Peter Stine whose names like his own means stone, and to somehow weave in a theme about cities a nest in his heart that has turned so hard and barren. The soul is like an eternal city, wrote Freud in his *Civilization And Its Discontents*, where as in Rome one has only to *"change direction to find a different view."*

There was another belated Cinco de Mayo show on the last afternoon at Highland Elementary, and Mrs. Herman had left a sheet for the asphalt. Each class was assigned a little spot around the yard for the performances, and the afternoon was bathed in a California light while everyone came together for a good time.

"Stay by me now," said the old male sub to the frisky cubs while their mother was gone, and after two days of his love they followed him through the maze as if by scent. He felt like one of them and pretending they were now the family he had always wanted he walked with them almost proudly and spread the sheet for their place in the sun, the lines of Traherne echoing from all the glowing faces in the yard, *"The boys and girls were mine and O how did their lovely faces shine. . . .I knew not that they were born and should die but all things abided eternally as they were in their proper places . . . from everlasting to everlasting. . . .Eternity manifest in the light of day and the city in Eden."*

Look, said Traherne and the Oakland Public School District, look through a window washed clean with children and all their little egos on parade, the little Latinos showing off with *La Cucaracha* and the little Cambodians with their "Umbrella Dance."

But they were not in Eden or even in Mexico or Cambodia, they were on 85th Avenue in East Oakland, and the sun, at first warm and pleasant, had become too hot and the dances too long.

"Can I go to the bathroom?"

"Yes, go ahead."

"Can I go too?"

"Yes, go ahead."

"Can I get a drink of water?"

"Yes, get a drink of water."

Then Amy and Megan found Denise, the librarian, sitting in a chair in the shade by the wall and they went to sit in her lap. She was a middleaged woman with no ring on her left finger, and like the sub she was in love with them, though she was able to hug them close and not be charged with sexual abuse.

Look, said envy and empathy, look how close she hugs them and holds them to her heart.

"Come," said the wish to be like Denise, the librarian, "come, let's all go sit by her in the shade."

"There's no room."

"We'll make room."

And so for the rest of the afternoon they gathered around the two old folks who loved them, and even though he wasn't allowed to hug them close they sat on the sub's lap as well.

THE ARTIST'S MOTHER

I've longed for someone since I can remember and not a night goes by when I don't reach for her. It's been hell having something between my legs instead of nothing, but as my mother would say, we must make the best of what we have and not complain of what we don't.

She's back in the valley and I just returned from the long drive. It used to be every four weeks, but I made it three since she'll be ninety this year and I go as often as I can before one of us disappears. I once said it was for her sake, but I now admit it's for my own. She's a kick in the ass and I always look forward to it, my car packed with my laundry as if I were going home again.

"You still take your laundry to your mother's?" Joe said the other night when we warmed up for basketball. "That's disgusting."

"Why?" I said. "It's better than the laundromat, and anyway she wants it, it gives her something to do, she says my laundry is her happiness."

"That's disgusting," Joe said, "a man your age taking laundry to his ninety year old mother."

It's a pleasant drive after passing the windmills on Altamount, and except for when I was away I've been going and coming for twenty-years. When she lived back east I'd share a ride across country and when I lived in England I'd take a charter in the summer and write once a week the rest of the time. She's illiterate, but I'd write my English simple enough for a mailman to read. I was eighteen when I moved out and since she was from the old world she didn't understand why I didn't stay until I got married like my brother, yet she was always better than I at living alone. She never asked anything but that I keep in touch and I created the routine on my own.

Here I am, Ma, I would say, don't worry, I'm okay. I wasn't really, I was miserable as hell, but I would hate her worrying. Now when I want to tell her how miserable I am she tells me to shut up. "What do you have to be miserable about?" she says. "Be satisfied with what you have. Look at me, I'm satisfied. Whenever you're miserable, think of me and you'll be happy."

No, those letters weren't because I didn't want her to worry. Despite my need to cut the knot, they were to the only one who seemed to tie me to this planet. I was nineteen when I told her I was going to live in Mexico and write a book. "Don't worry," I said, "I'm taking a bus." Then I hit the road with my thumb out, and lo and behold who was the first ride but old Po-Po from the neighborhood who spilled the beans while I was sending postcards from Memphis and Houston: "I just got off the bus, Ma, and I'm now in the Greyhound Station." Since then she's learned never to believe anything I write.

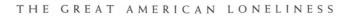

1NOV98

Sometimes I would love her so much I'd cry. In fact whenever I thought of her with love I'd cry as if she were gone and I'd never see her again, yet I used to have dreams where I yelled at her with such anger I would wake in a sweat. My dream mother was not her of course, but they were related somehow. Leave me alone, I would yell, go away! I've always loved her, but we've had our epic yelling battles. She's from the Mediterranean and could yell like Anna Magnani. Even her Italian pals in the factory would say she was like Anna Magnani because of her strong nose and flashing eyebrows.

I used to hate her yelling and am still attracted to women with soft voices, my femmes fatales not at all like her in looks or type except in their vibrancy. I love vibrant women. I also hate them. There's no one I hate more than a woman I love who doesn't love me back.

Where am I? Oh, yes, I was just passing the wind-mills on my way to old Z in the valley which is what I sometimes call her in my journal, Z for her name Zaroohe, which comes from Persia.

When I arrive at her home there's some ply-wood in the drive-way so the oil from my car won't drip on the cement, if it does she rushes with her wire brush as quick as Greenpeace in Alaska. She's one of the clean types and though I always appreciated her clean sheets and cozy home, her extreme tidiness could make me scream.

"I was always this way," she once said when she admitted it resembles a sickness. Even as a girl in the internment camp she always made her bed after waking each morning. Never once, however, did she ever ask my brother or me to make our own and we both scattered our mess wherever we wanted. When I was a child she even let me pencil my cowboys and horses on the wall by my bed as if it were a blackboard and when the weekend came she would scrub them away with *Babo* and let me make more. Some people are like this in our world, they just love to clean. I had my first wet dream when I was eleven and when she saw the gluey spot in the morning she lay a square cloth under the new sheet so the mattress wouldn't stain the next time. She'd wash that cloth too of course, but the stains would linger like mementos from all my dreamgirls.

After I pull in the the driveway I dump my laundry by the washing machine in the garage and she sorts the colors from the whites. She really does love to do it and not only because she loves to work, it's not just any laundry, it's her son's laundry.

"Of course," she says in her matter-of-fact way, "if you had a wife I wouldn't do this for you." But I don't take this matter-of-factly and with Joe's voice in the background my bachelorhood sinks into shame and failure. When I first left her I didn't want her washing machine or her food, I wanted to become a man and build my own home. Now I bring my sheets and take her jars not only because I don't like laundromats and enjoy her cooking, but because it makes her feel good. I wish I had a child whom I could feed and clean. It must be wonderful to be a parent. Remaining a bachelor son, however, can be so painful I want to die.

I used to think my death would be unbearable to her, but the older she grows the more enlightened she appears, and nothing seems to bother her except the ants in her kitchen. She might grieve like a Greek chorus should I die before her, but as she herself approaches death she accepts life in all its forms and wishes nothing but to go in peace without torture by a hospital machine. We sometimes hear how the approach of death can intensify life and bring a happiness to every last minute, and I see such a happiness in her when she hangs the laundry by her fruit trees and vegetable garden. To stretch her arms to her son's underwear by the blossoming apricot is everything, and she has no wish for anything more. Renoir once said of his own peasant mother, "Her laundry was as important as the German Empire." I imagine infants feel this way when they smile like Meher Baba who tells us not to worry and be happy. She often seems like a child now and like a Baba as well, an old Z who tells her old son not to worry, there's really nothing to worry about anymore.

She was not always this way of course. The vitality and the brightness, the Jimmy Durante twinkle and the strength of an elephant, was always in her, yes, but it was a hard road and I never tired of her turning it into a saga.

"Why do you tell people I never talked to you as a child," she once said in Armenian. "Before your father got sick I used to talk to you all the time. In fact one day Baidzar came up the stairs and heard me talking in our kitchen when you were not even a year old. 'Zaroohe,' she said, 'who were you talking to, I thought your husband went to work?' 'I'm talking to my baby,' I said, 'I always talk to him.'"

"I didn't say you never talked to me," I said, "I said you never listened." "Well, you're probably right," she said, "I needed to talk, but why do you complain about it, you can't have everything, be thankful I at least talked to you."

Nevertheless she feels a little guilty now and tries to correct herself. "So tell me," she will say, "how are things with you?" "Well," I start to say, "I. . . ." But before I can finish she says like a child, "I had a wonderful week, did you see my fava beans, how they sprouted so well?" I let her continue. She's alone even more than I and has so much she wants to tell me. As I've done since I was a baby I sit like an audience for her tales that go back as far as she can remember.

Alas, it is not far enough and she can't remember her own mother's face before the death march. She can remember her mother working hard like herself, but the face remains a blur, and it is this blur that feels like the word *mother* itself.

Mother: what does it really mean? How revolted I would feel when women used it with pride and selfhood. Like an old male who lost the rut to win a mate and must wander alone, I recoiled at so many females carrying bellies like an insect queen and then squirting into this fallen r e a l m more I's for an endless longing. Nor was my own mother pardoned from this horror where she was just another uterus for misery and death.

Yet the more my love deepens the less she is *mother* than simply Z, and with her I might learn what the word really means. She, however, knows herself only as a mother. As I became an artist, so too she must have become a mother when she was just a barefoot orphan on her own path through life, as if in needing a mother she had to become one herself. It was her way of joining life and it seems to have worked well regarding my brother who had a family of his own, but with me it feels different.

I used to think how much better off I was than the poor girl who lost her family in the desert and almost starved to death, who at sixteen had to marry an older man she had never seen before and had to sew in a factory twelve hours a day until it became eight when the union started, who when her first son was just an infant had to return to the factory and whose brief happiness was shattered when her second husband was crippled by a stroke, who when her second son was old enough for school had to return to the factory and care for a cripple and keep the refrigerator full and the sheets clean and the walls clean and everywhere clean because that's what being a mother meant, to feed and to clean and not complain about petty things. What a story, the story her boy kept wanting to hear as if the hardship were beautiful. What a hard life my mother had, he would think, how much better off I've been than she.

But I don't feel this way anymore, especially when I visit her wonderful home. She bought it when my brother moved his family to Fresno in '71. Before then her retirement plan was to buy a little house in Belmar on the Jersey coast about a hour from where he lived in Ridgewood. Unlike me, he always lived near her and because of this I could feel free to wander without the guilt of leaving her alone. Once my father's death freed her from doctor bills she started saving her pay and by the time she retired she had eighteen thousand dollars, which was just enough in those days. She chose Belmar because that's where the tribe would go in the summer and some like her best friend Manooshag had already retired there. Then my brother went through a change of life and decided to move to Fresno. I had come to Berkeley a few years before, so with her two sons in California she also came and bought a little house near my brother's in one of the developments that decimate orchards and fill them with monotony. I used to think it shameful, but regarding my mother the cul-de-sac couldn't be better. For the first time since she lost her parents she had her own home with no worries about heat or hot water. Ants yes, but she could handle them and the shopping center was just a short walk and she would learn the bus system like a survivor in a jungle.

"I don't move anywhere I can't take a bus," she said, "I'm not asking anyone to drive me around." She still takes them and just the other day rode downtown for her check-up at the clinic which told her she's "okay." It is her good health that makes me feel how fortunate she is and of course I mean her mental health as well. How did she get so healthy, I wonder, my own lungs now black from all my cig-arettes of despair?

One day while working in her garden she didn't see me looking when she lifted her skirt like a child to squat and piss by her grapefruit tree. It was then I fully realized who she was and where she had come. She was a peasant child who had been exiled to a factory for fifty years and now she was home with the sky and the earth. She herself once said casually as if it were just another fact, "They took away my father's vineyard but God gave it back to me."

By God she meant that which she always trusted and had nothing to do with a Jesus or DNA. If you ask her she'll tell you she's a Christian because to her being an Armenian is being Christian and how could she not feel Armenian when her family was slaughtered as such? But churches mean nothing to her except for funerals and her God is simply that which she never doubted. "You have to believe in something," she once said to someone who claimed to be an atheist. "It doesn't matter what, the sun, the sky, this lit-tle rock, but to believe in nothing is impossible." Once when someone talked about suicide in regard to a friend in a nursing home, she said: "It's easy to talk about it, but how could you kill yourself when your soul is so sweet?"

She's often wise when it comes to faith and her igno-rance is just as illuminating, though she would be angry at my making it public. She's as alert and inquisitive as ever, but I still can't convince her the earth is round or that there is a north, south, east and west. Calendars, maps, or any-thing Copernican is beyond her, yet she managed to raise two sons and provide a home until they were ready to build their own, her memory and sense of direction sharpened by her archaic psyche.

She is in short as natural as they come, or "grounded" as we used to say. When I asked her one day what she thought of cremation she said no, it didn't appeal to her, she wanted to be buried in the earth, as if to say her body, which she respects so deeply, should return to what she loves. Anyway, she had just bought a cemetery plot because it was on sale. She's one of those types that will walk a mile to save a nickel, and her eighteen thousand dollars didn't come easily.

It might give her mortal anguish to spend a nickel on herself, but her generosity is like one of her fig trees which gives such pleasure to her neighbors. She can't endure seeing food go to waste, especially in remembering the death march. She can be as frugal as a French farmer, but the five hundred dollars a month from Social Security plus the hundred from the union is more than she needs, so she always has some left over for her unemployed son. "I don't want it," I say, but she insists it's for the car to visit her. "What am I going to do with it?" she says, as if it were the figs she has to avoid because of their sugar.

One day she told me she could remember the mulberries falling on her face when she woke in the morning in her childhood. She and her parents and her two brothers all slept in the open from spring to autumn and she grew up playing among trees and vines. During the winter they all lived in one room in the city, but when the rains ended they would return to their vineyard and live like peasants since prehistory. This was in Adana by the Mediterranean where Turkey curves into Lebanon and the sun is as friendly as in California or Provence. Their faces remain a blur but she can remember her father tying the vines and her mother boiling fruit into syrup, the donkey sleeping under them and the mulberries as long as her finger.

In my darkness now I love to hear about them and search for new questions so she can tell me more. "Why are you asking me so many questions," she says, "are you writing a book?" "No," I say, "it's not for a book, it's because I like hearing about the *aki*. "*Aki* is her Armenian word for the vineyard and the sound of it evokes a lost Eden to me now, the home of my mother's childhood which gave her the roots she could transplant after she was exiled. The genocides and wars would come and go and she would endure because her roots would stay healthy and her arms would welcome life whatever it might bring.

No, I no longer think how much more fortunate I have been. I know how to read and I know the earth is round and I know north, south, east and west, but I don't know what she knows and I don't even know how to sew. I strived for success since I was a boy and yet what have I done compared to her? With nothing but the grace of her God she raised a family and built a home and what have I done but wander in loneliness while longing to go home again?

During the old days all that psychology stuff tried to tell me it was because of my mother I was neurotic, it was because she abandoned me when she returned to the factory or held on to me in her loneliness, but it's all baloney now and even if it were true it wouldn't matter anymore. Nothing really matters but here and now and letting go of whatever holds us down. And I don't, I don't let go, especially of her, I still hold on to her, I still bring her my laundry, I don't want to lose her. She's all I have, I feel sometimes, when she goes there's no one and I will be like a kite let loose in the wind and never come down again. Often in my flying dreams I am rising in an overwhelming thrill and then in panic at never coming down I reach for a roof or pole to keep me grounded and maybe I once reached for a mother like that, for without her I might have never come back. Or maybe to stay I would have married one of the women who would have said yes instead of rejecting them because none was the true love of my longing, I would have married like my brother and I would have had a home and family like he and Joe and all the others I have envied, but no, I did not have to let go of my longing, I could go on longing and longing and whenever I flew too far to return I could write Dear Ma on a postcard or bring my underwear to her washing machine and she would always be there with her roots in the earth and her smile like a Baba. Without her, I think, I would not have become an artist.

Or perhaps I would have become a different kind of artist. I used to think my becoming an artist had to do with

my father who sat like a crippled Hephaestus after Aphrodite had gone away, indeed he had been before his stroke a jeweler of delicate chains. Since I was a male I could not be like my mother though she was stronger than he, so instead I would be a cripple like my father and turn my pain into art. Yet who knows how anyone becomes an artist or anything else? I had genes for drawing and maybe even writing too, but my brother had even more and took a different road by wanting to work an ordinary job and live a simple life. I on the other hand thought only of how I could avoid work to have all the time I needed to become an artist.

There was no question of becoming anything else, it was the only way to survive. Already at five with no one home but a dumb cripple and a mother always gone, I was on my own in the wild city where the only way to survive was by longing for the sky as if someone were there. So off I went down the cliffs to the barges on the river like a little Wordsworth encountering the deep as if it were alive, always self-indulgent and fearless because come dinnertime I could always go home and the food would be warm on the table and the sheets would be clean, I could go anywhere I wanted and do whatever I wanted because I had a strong mother who never said no and who let me draw on the wall despite her obsessive cleanliness. And I stayed that way for the rest of my life, always wandering and searching and longing, yet what was I longing for but the very warmth back there by her side? Then why did I leave in the first place? Why didn't I just stay?

I couldn't of course, or I would have really become like my father. No, I am not a cripple, a healthy Zaroohe is in me somewhere, but I get lost, I get lost quite often and am like that little kindergarten boy after school one day when he hadn't quite learned the long route through the perilous city and stood on the corner crying until Donald Negrini, the butcher's son, came and led him through the strange streets.

I've been getting lost like that a lot lately, especially in the waves of homelessness that engulf our venal and profane America. If I can't find a job and pay the rent, what am I going to do, where am I to go? No one's going to buy anything I paint and Donald Negrini is nowhere to be found. Could I live with my mother again?

"No," she said in her matter-of-fact way, "I don't want you to live here."

I was a little shocked until I realized what she meant. She's been losing her balance and has fallen several times while working in the garden. Fortunately she was able to cushion herself with her huge thighs, but she's afraid that if I came to live with her she wouldn't be able to clean my mess anymore. It's all she can do to care for herself now and not burden anyone.

Yet whenever I visit she is still the same Zaroohe with her washing machine and her *dolmah* that gets better and better, her sheets as clean as always. I sleep in the room near hers and once when I woke first I looked at her in bed with her legs sprawled and her arm out and I loved her so much I started to cry.

Why was I crying when she was lying so alive? Why does love make us cry as if like children we are at the mercy of forces beyond our beseeching? I was crying as if I were a child who has lost his mother, but she was no longer the old woman who woke and peed and washed her face and then joined me in the kitchen.

"Did you sleep well, my son?" she asked. "I . . ." I said, and then she finished my sentence for me. "I slept good myself," she said. "I had a good dream."

My own dreams are stormy and dark, but hers are often peaceful and filled with light. Sometimes she sees my father and they kiss and love each other. Most of the characters are dead since she's the last of the old gang, but they come and go like visitors. Then one morning she said as if she had an vision, "I saw my brother, my son! I saw his face! I could see his face so clearly! 'Boghos,' I said, 'is it really you?' 'Yes,' he said, 'It's really me.'"

It was the first time since he disappeared in the desert eighty years ago. For eighty years his face had been a blur and now suddenly it was clear again. He was her older brother and she had often told me how she remembered him always drawing.

"What did he look like, Ma?" I asked. "How can I tell you that?" she said. "I know what he looks but how can I describe him to you?"

As she said this he became a boy by the river near the cliffs too far to see clearly, he and his mother and father and little sister all so far away, the more I tried to reach them the more they receded. "Ma!" I cried as a little girl once cried in a desert, "Ma!" Ma, as in the *mah* that meant death in Armenian and Ma as in Michelangelo's last *Pieta* where a crippled Christ returns to stone, Ma that was beyond any breasts or vulva and or a feminist selfhood about nature and the earth, Ma that had no gender or form but was the void that would be plenitude by letting go. Let go, let go, it said, don't be afraid, there will be light at the end of the darkness like a warm dinner for a boy back from adventuring.

So I returned to an old Z peeling apples at the table who was not my mother anymore, yet through her I might know the meaning of the word, though she could just as well have been a male. In fact she could pass for a male now, her great nose and wrinkles like an old Black Elk invoking a Grandfather.

In her bedroom there is on the wall facing her bed a picture of her second husband's father, one of my own grandfathers. She enjoys all kinds of pictures on her walls, and though she usually leaves the hanging to me, she wanted on the wall facing her bed the one of the old Pop with the Wyatt Earp mustache, his handlebars looking down at her as she sleeps every night. The picture is a tinted ten by fourteen blow-up my father had made of a little photo taken before the massacre. Unlike my mother my father had several photos of his family and he remembered his father well, so my mother knew more about him than about her own father. She loved her own father very deeply and I imagine she had substituted for his face the one of her old father-in-law with the grey mustache, though he was only in his thirties when he was slaughtered. She doesn't think like this of course, I doubt she looks at the picture except when she's cleaning the glass, but she has a father inside her and more than once while working in her garden she has turned to me and said, "I feel I have become my father now, I remember him shoveling like this."

So too as I sit here making lines have I become like my mother with her sewing machine. "My sewing machine is my *yo-yo*, "she once said. "You have your *yo-yo* and I have mine." *Yo-yo* is her way of saying yoga, which she calls my sitting on the zafu she had sewn and stuffed for me.

AMERICA

Rain now, and whatever word describes how the drops design the pane while this line moves across the screen, my little family (from *The Aki*) now back in the city for the winter, their tenement room like those in my journey through Asia with a water pump in a courtyard and the latrine nearby.

But even here in their humble room there is a warmth of those who are not alone and which my mother still has though she has been alone as long as I. How did she keep it and how have I lost it, the warmth of those Saturday nights when she would beg our landlord for hot water, "*Please, Mr. Camalingo, it's our bath night.*"

Then she would undress my father and ease him into the tub and when I was alone with him I would wash his hairy body that seemed so normal under the water. The bathroom was small but cozy and after we dried him I would hold his right arm which was limp from the stroke and help him slip it into the pajama sleeve. Then it would be my turn for the bath and after I was left to play in the tub my mother would come and drain the water and sit on the little stool and hold me between her legs to douse me with the brass pail from the porcelain bucket. Like all children I complained about the soap in my eyes but the exciting warmth of the water and her flesh was like the happiness I am trying to describe now. Then came the fresh pajamas still redolent of the wind and I would sit by the radio and trace with my finger the patterns in the carpet as the programs flowed like chapters in an epic, *The Lone Ranger* and *The Fat Man* and *Ozzie and Harriet* and *The Life Of Riley*. Not really, for they were on Friday nights, but I liked them more than those on my bath night. Then with my parents in the next room and my brother out late, I would snuggle under the quilt with my back to the window so the monster would not see my face when he climbed up the alley.

It is with this peaceful memory that my little peasants go to sleep in an old city long ago, their bedding like the futons now in vogue and their sheets washed with the soap my grandmother made from the ashes of the firewood, their bodies close together as the rain patters on the cobbles as it does here now on this windowsill.

I can't turn them into a novel like Tolstoy could with his own family, yet I too have always needed to write as if to go through a window into the rain, and it is with this need I would paint my mother who has always seemed a part of this life in which I've felt so alien and afraid. When I called her from my loneliness last night she was sitting just as alone but not at all lonely, and once again she wanted to talk as if to entertain a little baby in a high chair unable to answer. "Let me see," she said, "what else can I tell you?"

She didn't want me to be lonely, she didn't want her little boy to sit alone so far away, so after telling me about the different prices in the supermarket and the weeds that are starting to sprout by her fava beans, she paused as she searched for something else to keep the phone alive, then she said, "Oh yes, It's your brother's birthday in a few days, and when he dropped by this morning I gave him sixty-five dollars."

When we were all in Jersey she started giving each of us, including his wife and kids, a dollar for each year on our birthdays. She never knew her own birth date, but she had invented one for her passport and she told us how pleased she was when the bookkeeper in the factory gave her a present after discovering it in her file, so from then on we remembered it as well. There is a saying in Turkish that children born in March are wild and her mother would yell this saying whenever she was scolded. For some unknown reason she chose the fifteenth.

So too is it now March Fifteenth as my peasant family huddles in the tenement, and though they will not return to the *aki* this spring the scene is warm with her memory of her own bath in childhood, the women on Fridays and the men the next day and the big door of the *hamam* opening with an iron ring, the splash of water echoing through

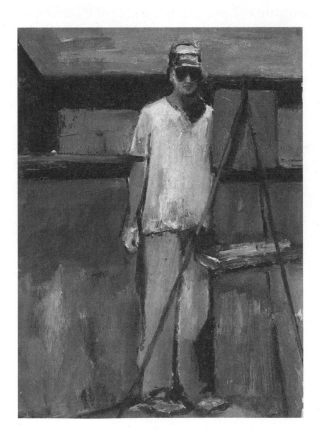

steamy halls and her own mother wrapped in a *footah* and bathing with her own bucket and bowl.

There was a little imitation *hamam* on Central Avenue in West Hoboken, or *pahn-niq* in Armenian, even though most of the immigrants had bathrooms by then. It was a kind of social club until everyone left for the suburbs. She took me there once when I was still young enough to be with the women and we bathed like she did with her own mother, then in the next room it was the grapefruit I remember most clearly, the women sitting in their *bur-noos* towels with gossip and laughter and the cool juice so refreshing after the hot steaminess, the white and yellow rinds as vivid as that neighbor tarring a leak on his roof.

My brother, Tom, can remember the bathhouse much better than I, for he went there as a teenager. We rarely talk, but I coaxed this out of him once. It was, he said, on the second floor of a duplex, and the men like the women would make *kef* with music and food, except they would have whiskey instead of grapefruit. He would go with his own father, Vahan, who like my father was in his fifties then, and they both loved the oriental music with the big bellied oud and the brass *dumbag* and the wild violin and clarinet. The music was not in the bath of course, but they are combined here for art's sake. It was called "oriental" music and my brother loved it as he loved the American music of his teenage years in the Forties. He was born in '29 when the immigrants were young enough to make *kef* as much as they could, and his childhood was as full of this *kef* as the big band music from his American culture, the story of my brother's life like the story of America where the old music would flow into the new like *kef* into Benny Goodman and Frank Sinatra.

In fact, my brother is America, or rather what America is all about, he is why our parents were shipped here from war and genocide. I, however, am the ghost America, as in the second *ghost* sheet after printing a monotype, I am the other America unfulfilled and wanting something different. My brother made a life of looking on the bright side and playing by the rules in order to have it. He was gifted with more intelligence and talent than I, yet he did not want to be intelligent and talented, he did not want to stand out and be different but to be one of the gang, and when his turn came to get a job and build a family he worked as hard as the next guy and did not complain, for all he wanted was to come home and listen to music and make *kef* on the weekends, just like his father. But lo and behold, things did not turn out as America said they would and in the second half of his life there were no bathhouses where he could bang the *dumbag* and drink a few. What had happened, where was that glow of togetherness when he was a boy?

"Are you coming for Christmas?" he asked when he dropped by our mother's home while I was there. Every Christmas since he moved to Fresno he has a get-together with his family and his pals, but I would not always come. "I don't know," I said. "Do you think I should?" "Why not?" he said. "Just come and have a few drinks and get a little high, it's no big deal." We have never been close socially, but his idea of family is stronger than its fact. He still wants me to be like his idea of an uncle for his kids who are past thirty already, and in his own kind of loneliness he still looks forward to making *kef* again. No, I should backspace, for I don't know what he thinks or feels, I project inside his outline my own wish to be just an ordinary guy with a simple happiness.

He was not yet five when Z left his father and took him to the little apartment she had found two blocks away, and it would be a few years before she would get together with Armenag, who was to become my father. In one of her little vignettes about my brother's childhood, which I often love more than my own as if they are more real, she said the apartment was not the one on the top floor where I grew up but on the first floor where she had only the front rooms because the older of the landlord's kids slept in the back.

She was only thirty then, she and her little Tommy in a humble apartment like innocent peasants protected by life for the purpose of making more of it. It was at the end of summer when she separated from his father and she had to plead with the principal to enroll him in the school around the corner because he wouldn't be five until December. Then in the morning before she went to the factory she took him there with a little oriental rug for his nap, the same little rug on my rocking chair here in this cottage, then after school his grandmother would take him to her own home until he could join Z after she finished work. "But he never once slept there," she would always emphasize, "he always came home for dinner and slept with me." She felt some guilt of course, and even to this day she still feels a tinge of it, but as if to compensate for his broken home she always adds how well his father and grandmother

treated him, while she herself gave him as much as she could. Then would come the summers when she would lock the door and take him on the train to Binghamton in upstate New York.

She had an "uncle" in Binghamton, her mother's first cousin, Petros Bidinian, who had fled from Hadjin to escape the Turkish draft which made slaves and cannon fodder out of Armenian young men. When she herself arrived in America she found this Petros and he had a little business in what was then a farming community where he and his family lived on a little *aki* of their own.

She would talk of those Binghampton summers more happily than all her other adventures in life. It was not easy for her to go up there, yet she went not just for my brother but herself as well. It was during the Depression and the factory did not pay enough for a two month vacation on a farm, so she must have been resourceful and determined. She was not about to leave her son in a hot apartment with her mother-in-law all summer, and Binghampton may have reminded her of the *aki* in her childhood.

"When we returned in September," she still says with a happy gleam in her eyes, "I would have just a few pennies left, but I would have bags of vegetables and corn and Tommy would be chubby from eating so much all summer." Then she would remember the fresh milk and eggs and the clean air and how much fun they had at the swimming hole. Her uncle's wife Marquhi was close to her age and they became best friends, the single mother Z staying home with the eight kids while Petros and Marquhi ran their drycleaning shop in town.

It was the summer of the big family happiness, and here now it fills in for the one with my humble peasants. I didn't know the Bidinians as my brother did, they moved to Pasadena in '41, a year after I was born, but I had my own summer with them in '52 when my mother and I took the

Greyhound west after my father died. My brother had been drafted because of the war in Korea and once again a single mother locked the door and took her second son on a *vacation*, from *vacatio*, for freedom. It was the first time I had crossed the Mississippi or even the Delaware, and as I turned twelve my hormones were as wild as the expanding landscapes.

There was no *aki* in Pasadena and all the Bidinian kids were adults by now, so there would be no cows and orchards like in Binghampton, but I got a little taste of a big family happiness anyway. Uncle Pete and Aunt Marquhi spoke only Turkish like all the Armenians from Cilicia, and Z enjoyed speaking it again. It was her mother tongue and the only one she knew until she learned Armenian in the orphanage. Speaking Turkish in her uncle's house may have been all that was left of her childhood.

He was a very short and powerful Napoleon kind of paterfamilias who sat at the head of the table and downed the hottest jalapenos without a blink. He had come to this country penniless in another version of survival, and he now owned several properties and drove a big '49 Buick with his head just high enough to see out of the windshield. "When he first proposed," Marquhi once said, "I almost laughed in his face because I was taller than he and his pants were too long for his short legs."

But she was herself an orphaned refugee with no other choice, and she grew to love him after he treated her like a queen. In Pasadena they lived at 1924 East Washington Street, and my mother slept on the other bed in Gracie's room while I had the other one in Fatso's. Fatso was really Richard and he was not really fat, but everyone had nicknames in this fun-loving family. He was my brother's age and had not been drafted for some reason like Chubby, whose real name was Charles, and it was on Chubby's bed that I slept. Liz and Tootsie and Tory were married with kids in other cities by now, but they each visited that summer. Gracie, the youngest, was going to Pasadena Junior college, and I was in love with her.

Duke, or Harry, slept out back in the spare room behind the garage, but he was not always at the dinner table and he slept until the afternoon because he was a gambler and came home from "work" at dawn. Yet he was the same as the others to Z, and she was equally fond of them. They were her younger cousins who called her "Auntie" and the only she knew at the time. Harry simply had, in her eyes, a different kind of job. "He was always different," she once said. "Even in Binghamton when he was boy he used to say he was not going to work like other people, he was going to figure out a better way to make money." He was a quiet generous man who would win great sums of money and then lose them all, and I wouldn't realize until I faced my own darkness that there was something different behind his warm and friendly eyes from the rosy picture I wanted to paint of his family's happiness.

They all had those same warm and twinkly eyes that seemed to always smile like the way I felt that summer, Pasadena so different from the world I had left in the hot and humid east. There was no smog then and the dry delicious weather was, I would later learn, much like Adana's. Pasadena was in those days a quiet spacious town of people like *Ozzie and Harriet*, and when I went to the baseball field the other boys welcomed me as if I were an American as well, they even let me join the league and gave me a T-Shirt and cap, then Uncle Pete, who despite how much he loaded the refrigerator was notoriously tight, even bought me a baseball bat. I had come not only to my mother's cousins who seemed like special beings to deserve this wonderful life, but to an enchanted California so different from the one I know today.

Even years later in '60, after I failed to settle in Mexico, I took the bus to Tijuana and hitched north to Pasadena as if it were an oasis. When I arrived in Altadena, the next town, a cop picked me up at three in the morning and drove me the rest of the way to 1924 Washington because the busses had stopped. I didn't want to wake anyone, so I lay on the front porch intending to wait until sunrise, but I fell asleep and the next I knew Marquhi was nudging me awake. She hadn't seen me since I was a kid and she thought I was a bum. I stayed about a week until I was rested enough to hitch to San Francisco where I was going to settle in North Beach, but I couldn't endure the fog in my summer clothes and I lay with a fever in a cheap room on Columbus Avenue until I was strong enough to hitch back to Pasadena. Again I rested until I was strong enough to hitch east to Jersey, but when I got as far as Utah I lost my traveler's checks and came to a little train station in the middle of nowhere with only twenty-five cents in my pocket. The office woman sent a collect telegram to my brother's shop in Manhattan, but he was on vacation and the shop secretary sent a telegraph check in his last name, so I couldn't cash it. I couldn't keep heading east with no money, but after I told the office woman I had relatives near Los Angeles she said a freight train was due in a few minutes and I could hop on if I stayed out of sight. I bought a loaf of bread with my last quarter in a little shop nearby and when the train arrived I hopped into an open car because the stars were so beautiful and surely we'd pass through the desert at night. Settling back with my loaf of bread and bottle of water, I looked up at the stars as if they were my angels and I must have been the most excited young man in the universe while the train rocked like a cradle until I fell asleep. When it stopped I thought we were in L.A., but one of the hobos in the yard said no, it was Las Vegas, and now all the cars were open and the desert was yet to come, the sun rising as the train started and I no longer singing its praise. It was June and I had no hat and by the time we reached Baker I couldn't take it anymore, so I jumped off as the train slowed through town, but I didn't know how to jump off a moving train and I injured my foot. Bruised and scraped I hobbled to a gas station to wash in the men's room, then I hitched the rest of the way and arrived in Pasadena again like a refugee. Fatso and Duke were gone by then and only Gracie was left with Uncle Pete and Aunt Marquhi.

She was six years older than I and the kind of woman I always wanted as a wife. She liked me too, but even if I were older I was not the kind of man she wanted to marry, she was in fact already married and divorced with an infant son,

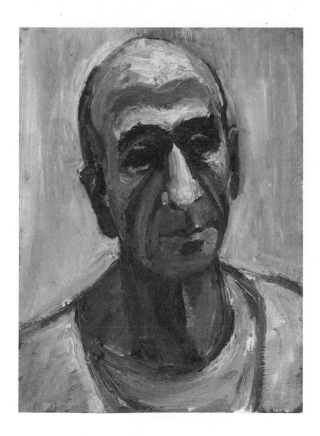

Randy, who would grow up troubled after she died of leukemia when he was not yet five, his father also disappearing in a fatherless America. Gracie had the sweetness of a nostalgic movie and though I knew her so long ago for such a short while I can still hear her voice and feel her warmth, yet if asked now as I ask my mother for dialogue, all I can remember her saying is: "Ugh, how can you use a handkerchief, it's so disgusting!" I blew my nose with handkerchiefs in the those days when tissues were still new. As we talked in the lovely Pasadena evenings she felt like a Sheherazade with her voice so sweet and her eyes so beautiful, yet all I can remember is her remark about my handkerchief. I was living in London when she died, and the news had opened a wound in my heart which had become so scarred and closed.

She died in the middle of the Sixties and by then Pasadena was covered by smog. Her father, Uncle Pete, died a couple of years earlier, and her little Randy grew up with his grandmother who, still grieving for her baby Gracie, gave him anything he wanted. By the time Randy was a teenager Ozzie and Harriet had long been gone and he grew up with a drug crowd, but fortunately, after heaping many troubles on his grandmother's head, he turned himself around and landed east, near Binghamton of all places, and he started raising a family of his own. I saw him for the first time since he was a child when we were all in Pasadena to be at Marquhi's deathbed.

Old Marquhi took a while to die, for her will to live was very strong. She was about ninety-three then and still holding on. Unlike my mother she couldn't stand to be alone and always had to have someone in the house. Tootsie, now divorced, came to live with her, and Chubby lived next door with his wife and disabled daughter. Liz and Duke were also just a few blocks away. Fatso was now living in Hamden recuperating from the surgery on his brain tumor and he came up and stayed with Liz. Tory came down from Sacramento with his wife in their Winnebago. They were all there when my mother and I arrived after I had picked her up in Fresno and drove her over Tejon Pass, Pasadena by now full of Mexicans and the new Armenians who had fled the wars in the Middle East.

Even Liz's son, Rick, was there after flying in from Arizona. I hadn't seen him since he was a teenager who thought I was an exotic longhair from Berkeley, but we liked each other despite the war. He was an All-American young man who had survived flying a helicopter in Vietnam and was now flying commercially. I always liked to look at his face which had those beautiful Bidinian eyes with the Huckleberry freckles of his Scotch-Irish father from Virginia. In fact all of the Bidinian grandchildren had their Armenian genes Americanized by their parents marrying into the new world, including Gracie, whose son, Randy, arrived soon after my mother and me.

Randy had been a long-hair while Rick was in Vietnam, and the Bidinian family had its share of fights about the war, but the war had been over for many years and here now by Marquhi's deathbed everyone was quiet and polite. The bed was in the living room where we could gather round and then return to the kitchen and dining rooms, my mother cheering everyone up with her usual ebullience. She had been a great support for Marquhi when Gracie died and she now stood by the dying Marquhi herself. Then Marquhi whispered in her ear for some *gilly-gilly shorbah* one last time. It was a peasant soup with little balls of bulghur and *gilly-gilly* was a nickname the kids gave it back in Binghampton, so my mother sent Fatso to the market and then cooked it once more. I drove that night to West L.A. to sleep at a friend's. When I returned the next morning Marquhi was still alive and would remain so for another two weeks, but some of us couldn't stay that long. Randy could stay only a night and had to fly back the next afternoon.

He hadn't seen his grandmother for quite a few years, partly because he couldn't afford to and partly because he had drifted away like an orphan who would sink roots somewhere else. He wouldn't have been able to come this time either, had the family not sent him the plane ticket. He was still Gracie's son and like a lost child deprived of the big family happiness he had a special place in old Marquhi's heart. "I want to give him some money," Marquhi whispered into my mother's ear, "I want to give him some money to take back with him."

But he didn't hear this. He had been out arranging his way to the airport and when he returned I was standing in the corner of the room watching the little drama unfold by the deathbed. Everyone still remembered when he was a kid who had stolen from his grandmother because of drugs, but now he had kids of his own, so my mother got the money and slipped it into Marquhi's hand.

I myself thought of the time when Randy was a teenager who had planted marijuana in the backyard. "Look," Marquhi had said to Z when she had been visiting, "there are some kind of volunteer plants in my garden, I think they will be flowers of some kind, why don't you take a seedling and plant it in your garden when you return to Fresno?" So with the Fresno sun and my mother's care it had grown into a giant bush while she kept watching for flowers. Then one day she got an anxious call from Marquhi. "What did you do with that plant?" Marquhi had said. "Oh, it's doing great," my mother said proudly, "but I don't see any flowers yet." Then Marquhi told her that Chubby's policeman friend had looked over the fence and noticed what was on the other side. So my mother pulled hers out and threw it in the garbage. Unfortunately I had arrived just after it was collected and only the crumbs remained. I didn't smoke it anymore, but I had swept enough to fill a bag and after I gave it to some friends in Berkeley they said it was the best they had in years.

As I stood by Marquhi's deathbed I watched as my mother put the money in her hand and then gestured for Randy to come closer. "Here, Marquhi," my mother said, "here is Randy." Then she held Randy's hand and pulled him closer to his grandmother. "Come, Randy," my mother said, "come closer."

It was all happening very quickly and when Randy approached thinking it was just to say farewell my mother suddenly joined his hand with her dying friend's and realizing it was full of money he broke into tears like all of us when we are suddenly loved after feeling abandoned. It was not only his old grandmother loving him with her love for her lost daughter but his own mother herself, and I was crying not only for him and for Gracie but out of a pain too deep to fathom and I had to leave the room or I would have fallen apart myself.

My mother however was smiling and she kept smiling even after we said goodbye and headed back to Fresno. She smiled that little smile that was both sad and happy at the same time, and as we crossed over Tijon Pass she said, "I'm glad we went, I'm glad I was able to say goodbye to my old friend."